AF597332

Fiona Rae
Row Paintings

DCV

Buchmann Galerie Berlin

Fiona Rae

Row Paintings

With an essay by / Mit einem Text von Terry R. Myers

A Row is a Row is a Row

> *And so now one finds oneself interesting oneself in an equilibration, that of course means words as well as things and distribution as well as between themselves between the words and themselves and the things and themselves, a distribution as distribution. This makes what follows what follows and now there is every reason why there should be an arrangement made. Distribution is interesting and equilibration is interesting when a continuous present and a beginning again and again and using everything and everything alike and everything naturally simply different has been done.*
>
> — Gertrude Stein, "Composition as Explanation"[1]

"Words as well as things and distribution as well." After such an example of Gertrude Stein's perfect—and ahead of its time—rhetorical and critical aim, what else can possibly be said about Fiona Rae's also pretty perfect and prescient *Row Paintings* that she started making in the late 1980s? It turns out there are many, many things left, because these are paintings that were in a robust conversation at the specific moment of their production, and they have kept that and other critical conversations going (again and again) in the thirty-plus years they've been in existence. I was introduced to Rae's work in 1994 in New York, with a group of paintings that stayed with me due not only to the uniqueness of their painterly energy and color schemes, but also because of the ways in which their compositions functioned. I do recall that those particular paintings were in conversation with abstract painting going on in New York at the time, for example, the work of Lydia Dona, Shirley Kaneda, Jonathan Lasker and David Reed (all of whom I was fortunate to know personally). More striking for me, however, was the connection they made for me at the time with the work of Los Angeles painter Lari Pittman. He and Rae were bringing something a bit different to the table, something that I didn't get until being introduced to these earlier paintings of Rae's, something that is basically happening right this very minute.

Words and things and distribution *right now*. In his studio in 1996, Pittman struck a massive painting of his over and over with his open hand while exclaiming that "it has a level of insistence that it's happening right now!, right, right, right now!!" (I have it on tape and the sound of the blows are everything.[2]) A couple of months ago Rae and I had a thorough conversation (virtually on Zoom, and I'll drop here that the pandemic's current warping of time and space fits my arguments perfectly), during which I was transported right back to the time of their making. Even so, however, these canvases also have more than enough of what they need to exist in the perpetual present that painting can often access seemingly without strain or surrender.

It is important to acknowledge that Rae introduced the *Row Paintings* in the infamous *Freeze* exhibition organized by fellow student Damien Hirst during his second year at Goldsmiths in 1988. As it was this show that was largely responsible for launching the absolutely refreshing phenomenon of the YBAs (Young British Artists), I now find it telling the level to which many of the works presented in it seem to me frozen in amber, trapped, if you will, in the specificities of their time and place. Rae's *Row Paintings* definitely and defiantly escaped, largely due to the simultaneity and malleability of the *triple entendre* they enunciate and embody.

So, in these paintings a row *is* a row *is* a row. There is no way anyone looking at them needs to be informed that they present their forms in regular rows on the canvas. They do so unapologetically, almost as if they are schooling us yet somehow not being didactic about it. (In other words, these paintings are anything but math problems to be solved.) Take, for example, *Untitled (nine on green)* (pl. 6). It can be seen as the most straightforward of the series: three rows of three eccentric forms that stick to the grid of the supporting greenish ground. Each of the nine forms is similar but not the same: according to Rae, they were created part by part by moving from one to the next, painting with the same type of stroke for each, then starting again with a different stroke, repeating the circuit until the picture's overall completion.[3] Rae also went to great lengths to diversify her brushes by, for example, screwing brushes together to make an awkward tool or heating them up in rabbit skin glue to pretty much ruin them. I believe such actions reinforce the interpretation I've had of Rae's work all the way up to its current state. Like many of the most important painters since at least Francis Picabia, she is committed to examining (and, importantly, playing with) painting's fundamental contradictions rather than picking a side. (She told me, while we were discussing Robert Rauschenberg's *Erased de Kooning Drawing*, 1953, that she always wants to be de Kooning and Rauschenberg at the same time.)

Those two artists share, like their spiritual and conceptual godfather Marcel Duchamp, a commitment to verbal language and its written form. De Kooning often started paintings by quickly painting large letter forms on the canvas (they are readable in some of his completed paintings), and Rauschenberg brought text directly onto the "bulletin board" of his surfaces as well as through using pictorial versions of language games like the rebus. All of Rae's *Row Paintings* function like presentations of letter forms, not readable as words or phrases but—as I've written before about de Kooning's paintings from 1956 to 1959—"each one functioning simultaneously as a painting and as a broadcast of painting itself."[4] This supports the noisy row of her paintings as they show themselves to be arguments for and against painting as well as amplifications of the painted strokes beyond categorizations like abstraction, figuration, beautiful and ugly. These are paintings that are having a row, not only noisily arguing against the short-sighted painting cancel culture of the late 1980s/early 1990s, but also, let's say, very much pleased with bickering amongst themselves.

By now it may not be all that surprising that while at Goldsmiths Rae wasn't familiar with the work of the New York painters mentioned above, but was well-versed in the 1980s text and graphic-design inspired work of Jenny Holzer and Barbara Kruger. (Rae had also been studying English Literature before switching to visual art.) Knowing this helps appreciate the underlying complexity of the compositional clarity of the *Row Paintings*, as well as the almost programmatic distribution of their shared terms from painting to painting. One of the earliest, simply named *Untitled* (pl. 8), isolates and stacks three abstract horizontal "vistas" as if they are on display in a shop window or performing on a stage. Moreover, each vista does nothing to obscure the variety of its components: ampersands and the British Pound symbol tussle with such things as furry creatures and ladders (or train tracks, or, in the case of other paintings, direct references to the work of influential artists like Philip Guston) as they have been placed across color-field worthy painted bands of color done themselves in a number of ways. *Untitled (fourteen on green and pink)* (pl. 1) has a pivoted composition 45 degrees to the right (east?), and its fourteen painted forms are even more creature-like; painting and now the cartoon broadcast of painting all at once (Rae told me of her important discovery as a student of the work of George Herriman), distributed in something like Stein's equilibration that can spawn the "continuous present" of which she speaks so clearly complexly or vice versa.

The last row is more likely the first. And in terms of language it might be the biggest stretch but I've come to see that as precisely the point. It's the elasticity that matters most. Row, as a verb ("to row") describes the strokes made in water to propel oneself from one place to another. Rae's *Row Paintings* have duration not all that different from a trip down a river in a row boat, no matter if they seem to be capable of also moving with the propulsion of a rotor blade or a rocket. The visual evidence (residue) of the strokes made to move these paintings reaffirms that they were very much enacted while the paint existed in a liquid form, or at least something more malleable than what they've become. Rae doubles down on this by leaving us exposed clues that many of the paintings were tilted on all sides so that some of the paint could drip in any direction, including those that in visual terms defy gravity. (See, for example, *Untitled (six on grey 1)* [pl. 2].) This is the row that delivers us, here at the end, to time. During our conversation, Rae mentioned a prior invocation of mine of the work of quantum gravity physicist Carlo Rovelli, particularly his declaration that a rock is a very slow event.[5] Paintings, then, are things that are much, much closer to a blink of an eye (which begs the question of what we are), but it is their ability to keep that blink right now, right, right, right now, that will surely always demonstrate the exceptional value of sometimes stopping in front of them.

Terry R. Myers

NOTES

1. Gertrude Stein, “Composition as Explanation,” originally published in 1926, as reprinted in *Selected Writings of Gertrude Stein* (New York: Vintage Books, 1990): 521–22.
2. “Lari Pittman In Conversation with Terry R. Myers,” originally published in 1996, as excerpted in Terry R. Myers (ed.), *Painting (Documents of Contemporary Art)* (London and Cambridge, Mass.: Whitechapel Gallery and The MIT Press, 2011): 117–18.
3. My conversation with the artist took place via Zoom on 27 March 2021.
4. See my “Make Way for de Kooning,” in *The Brooklyn Rail*, October 2011, available at https://brooklynrail.org/2011/10/artseen/make-way-for-de-kooning (last accessed 30 May 2021).
5. See Carlo Rovelli, *The Order of Time* (New York: Riverhead Books, 2018), and my essay “Katharina Grosse: I See What She Did There,” in *Gagosian Quarterly*, Summer 2020, available at https://gagosian.com/quarterly/2020/04/21/katharina-grosse-i-see-what-she-did-there/ (last accessed 30 May 2021).

Terry R. Myers is a writer and independent curator based in Los Angeles, and an editor-at-large of *The Brooklyn Rail*. He is the author of *Mary Heilmann: Save the Last Dance for Me* (2007) and the editor of *Painting: Documents of Contemporary Art* (2011). His most recent curatorial project was the survey exhibition *Candida Alvarez: Here* at the Chicago Cultural Center in 2017. He was Chair of Painting and Drawing at the School of the Art Institute of Chicago from 2013 to 2018.

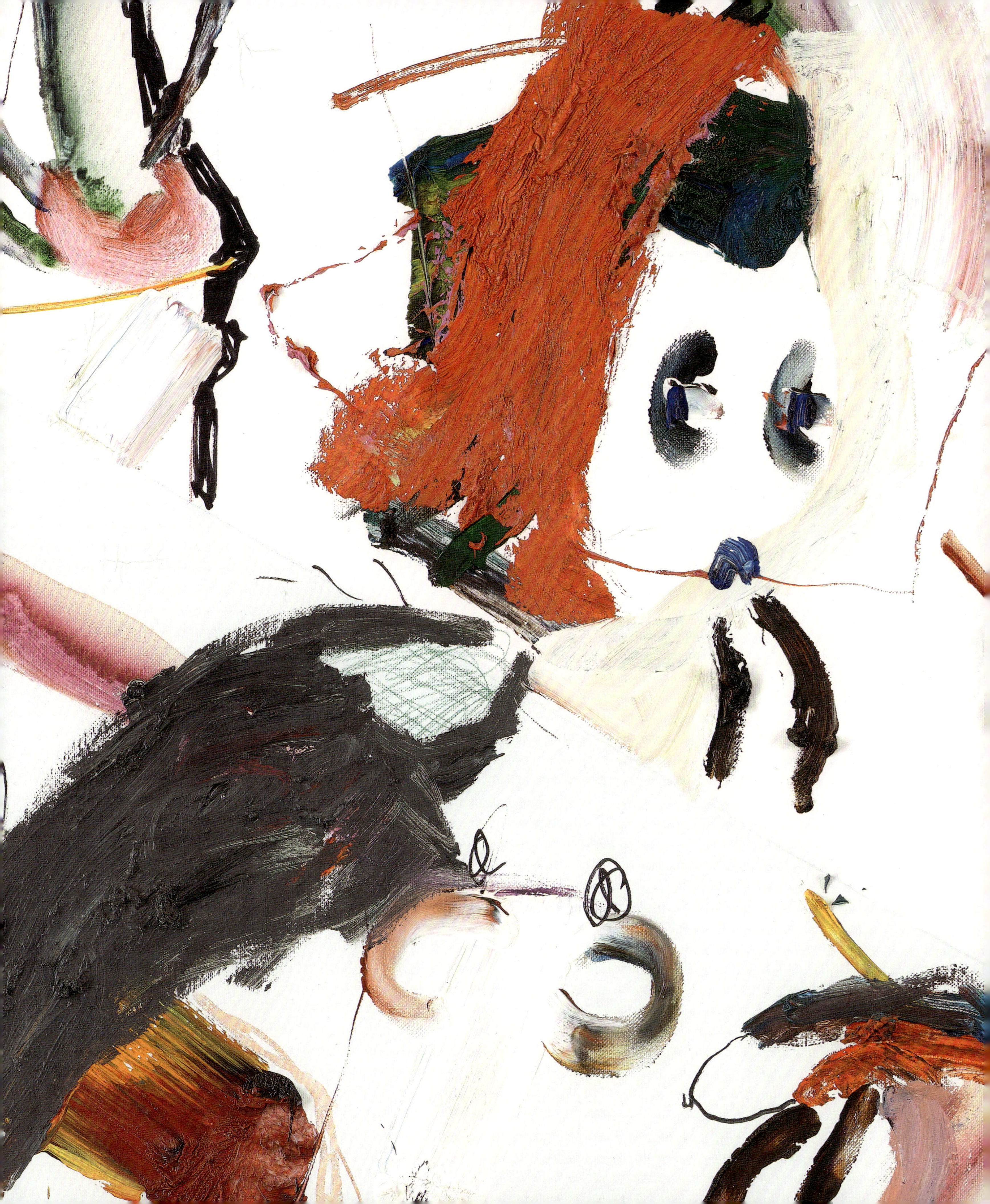

1

Untitled (fourteen on green and pink), 1989
Oil and felt pen on canvas
127 × 109.2 cm | 50 × 43 in

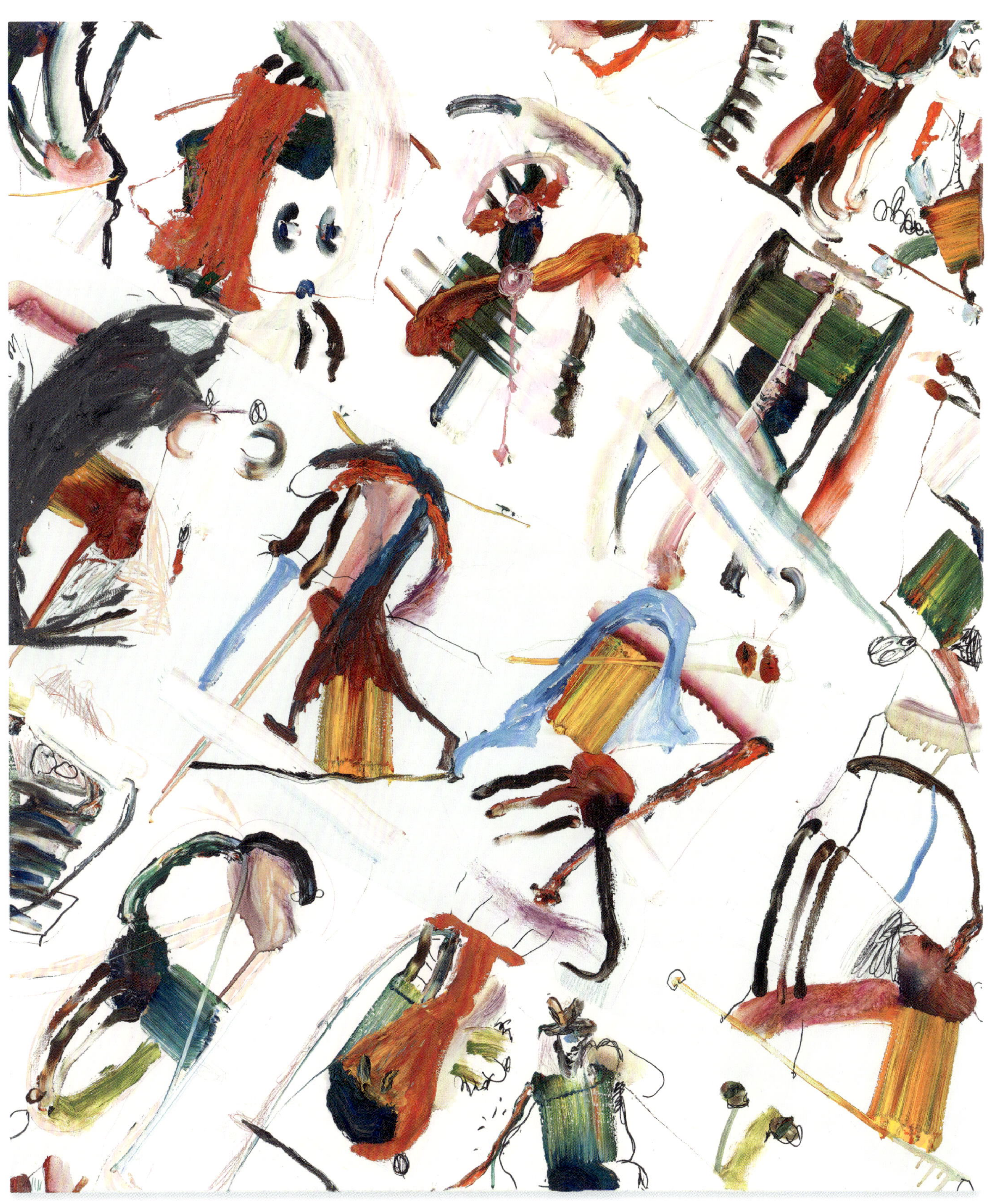

2

Untitled (six on grey 1), 1990

Oil on canvas

213.4 × 198.1 cm | 84 × 78 in

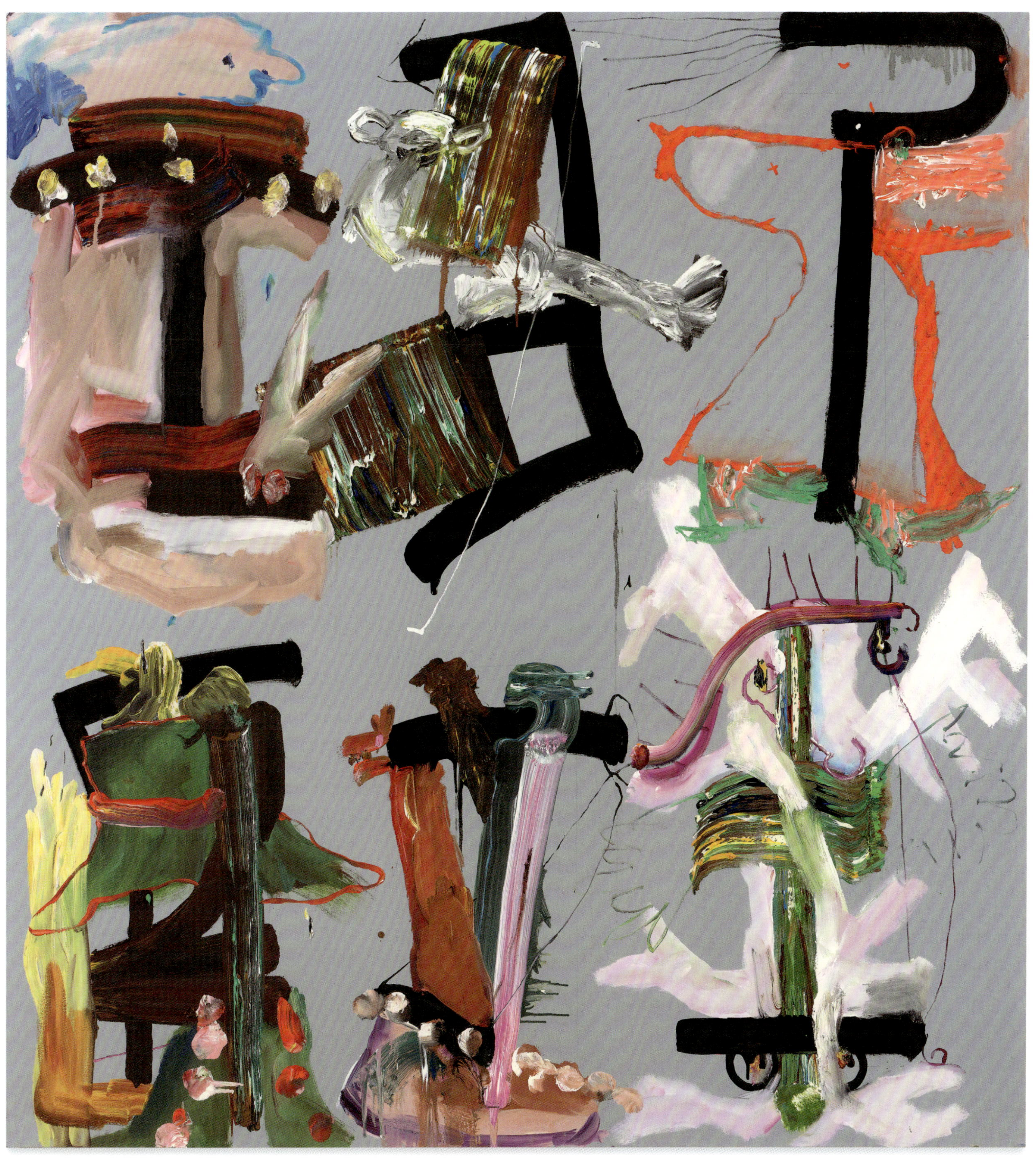

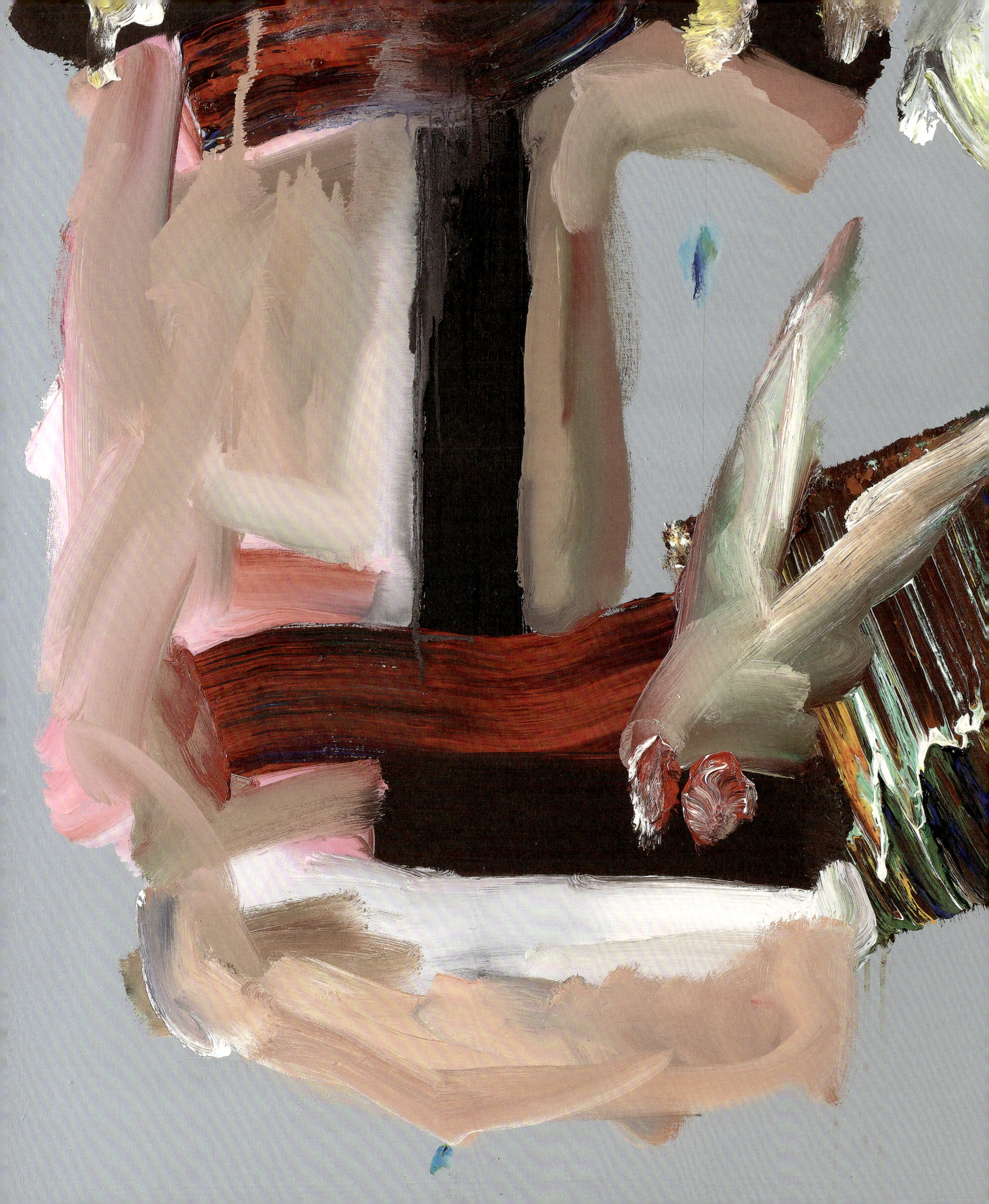

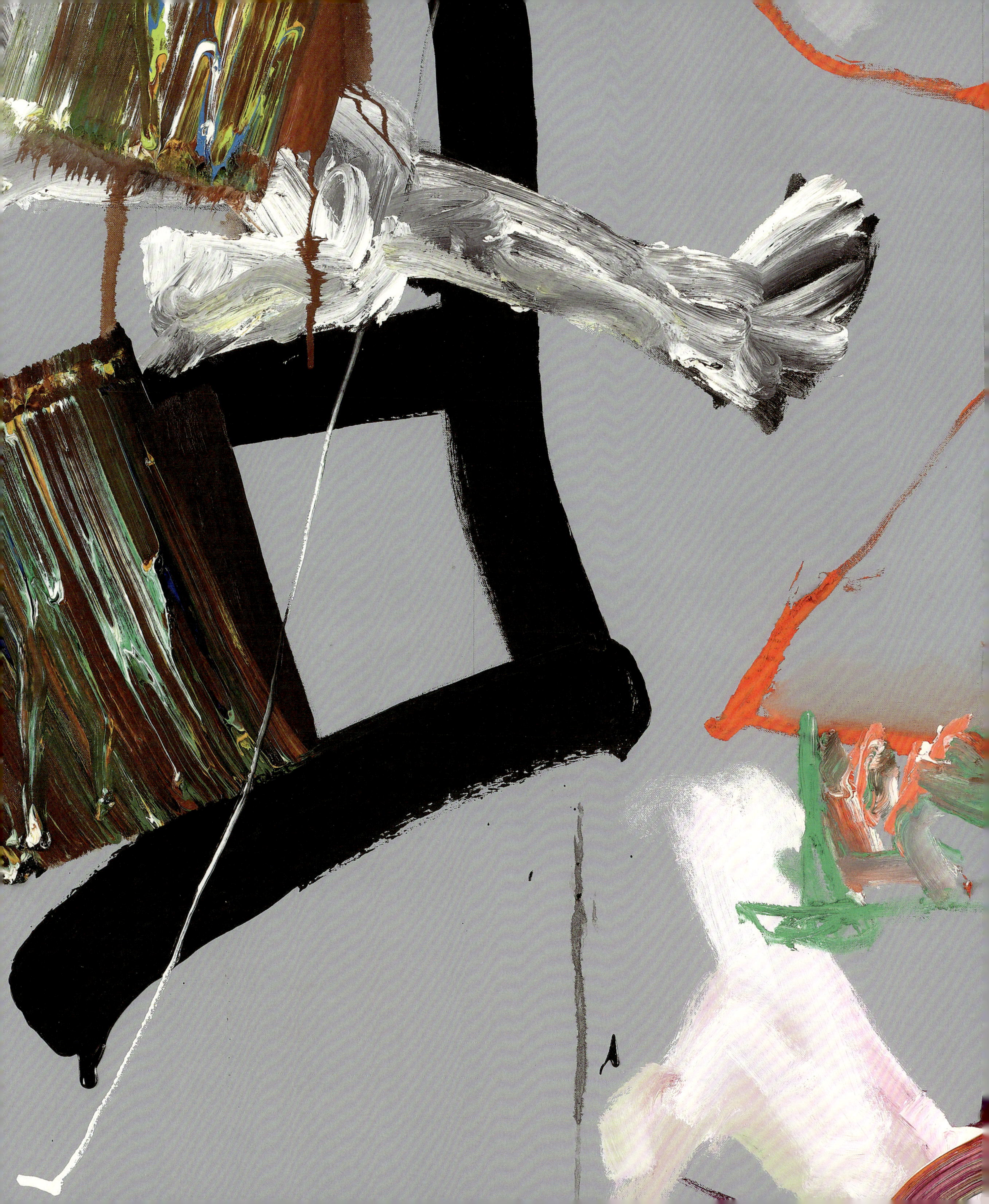

3
Untitled (six on pink and yellow), 1989
Oil on canvas
213.4 × 198.1 cm | 84 × 78 in

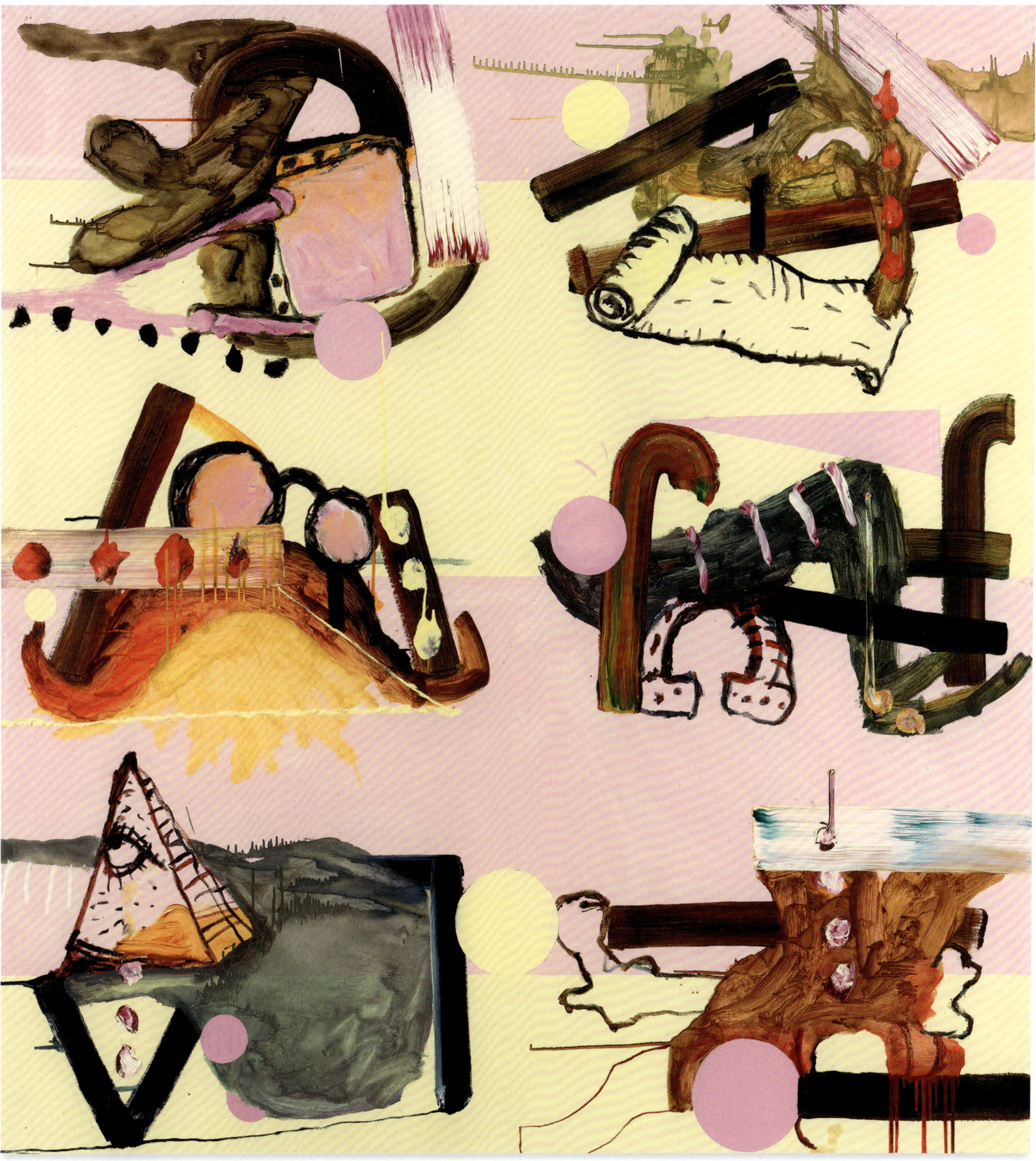

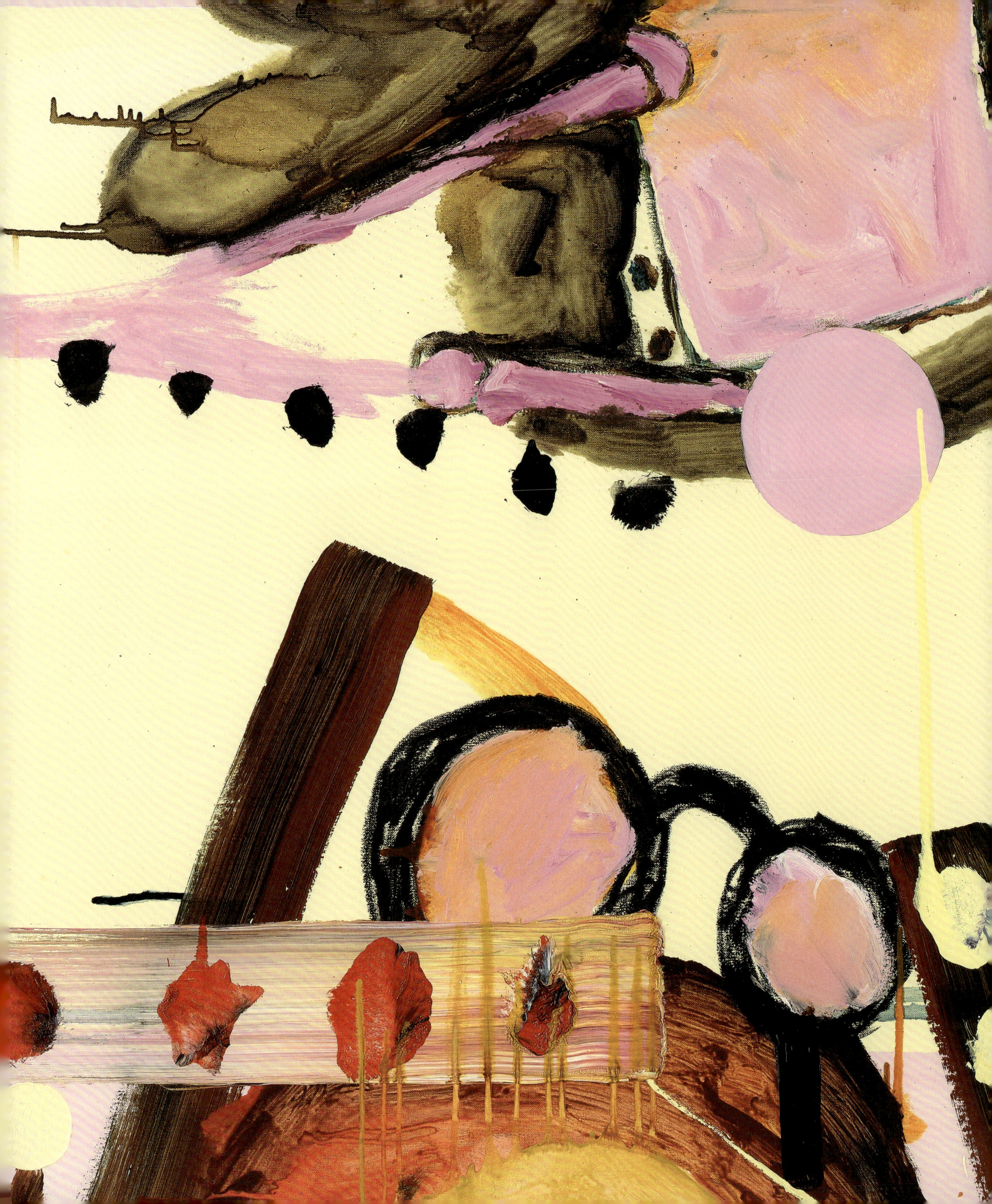

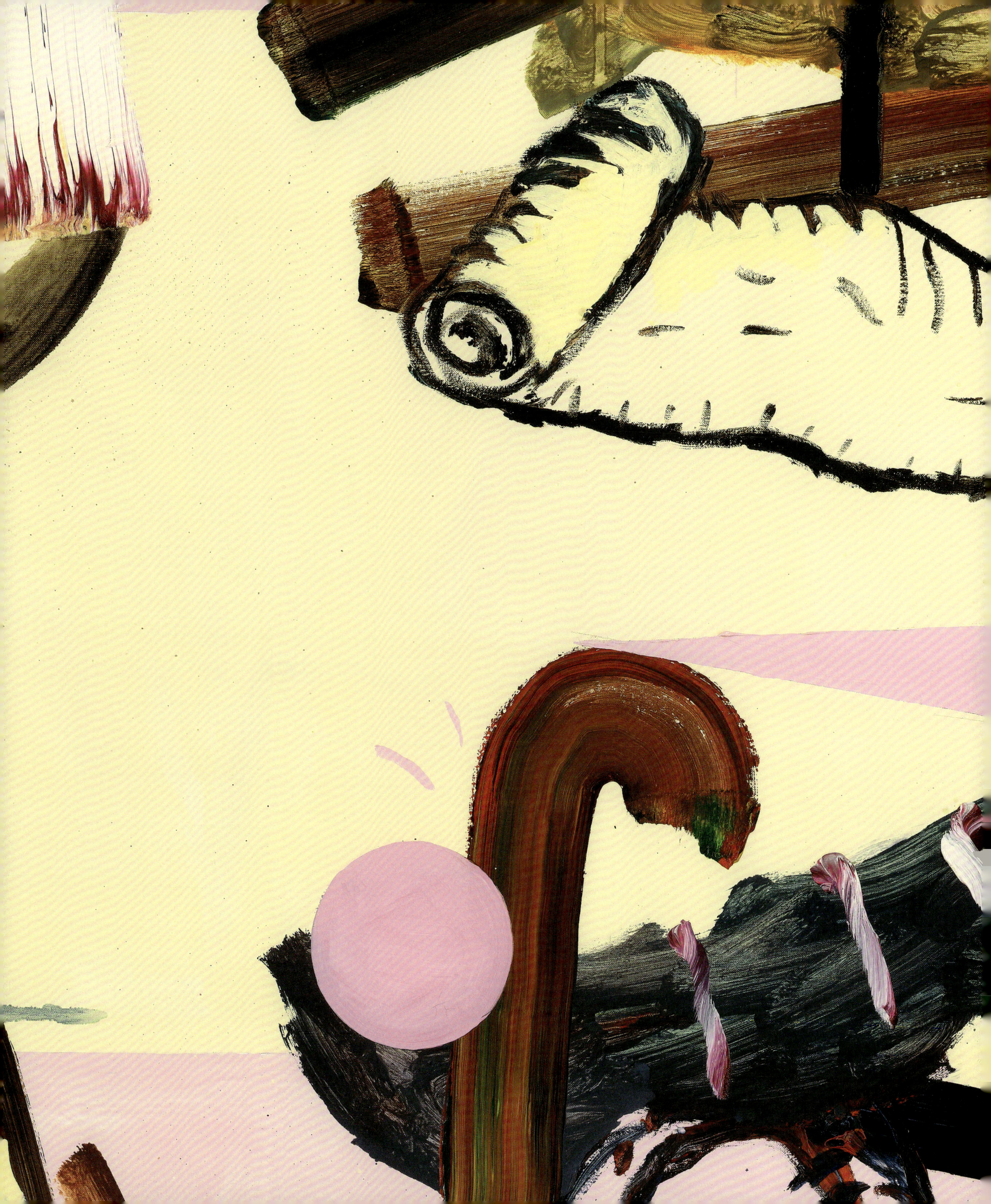

4
Untitled (twenty on two pinks and yellow), 1989
Oil and pencil on canvas
213.4 × 198.1 cm | 84 × 78 in

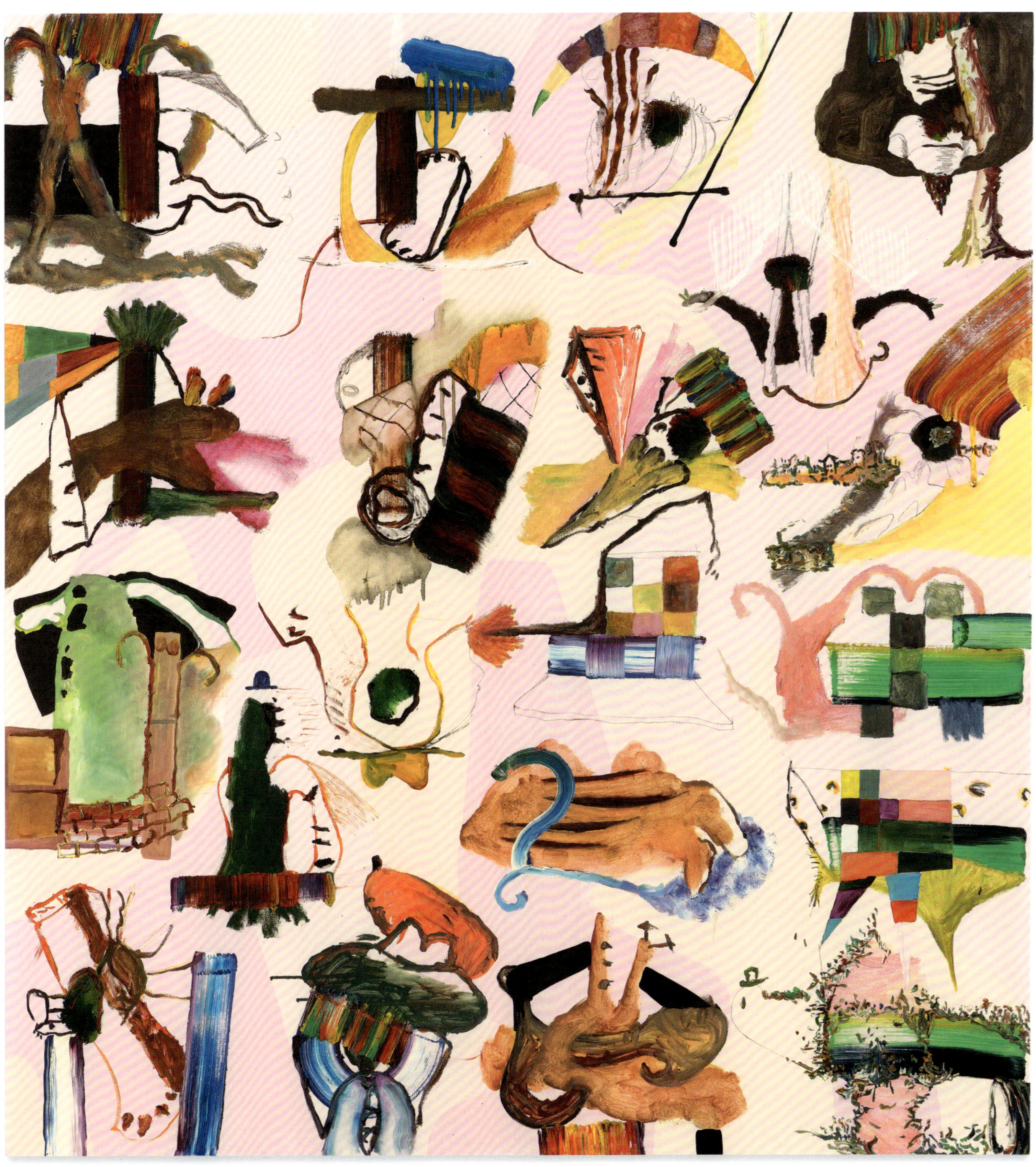

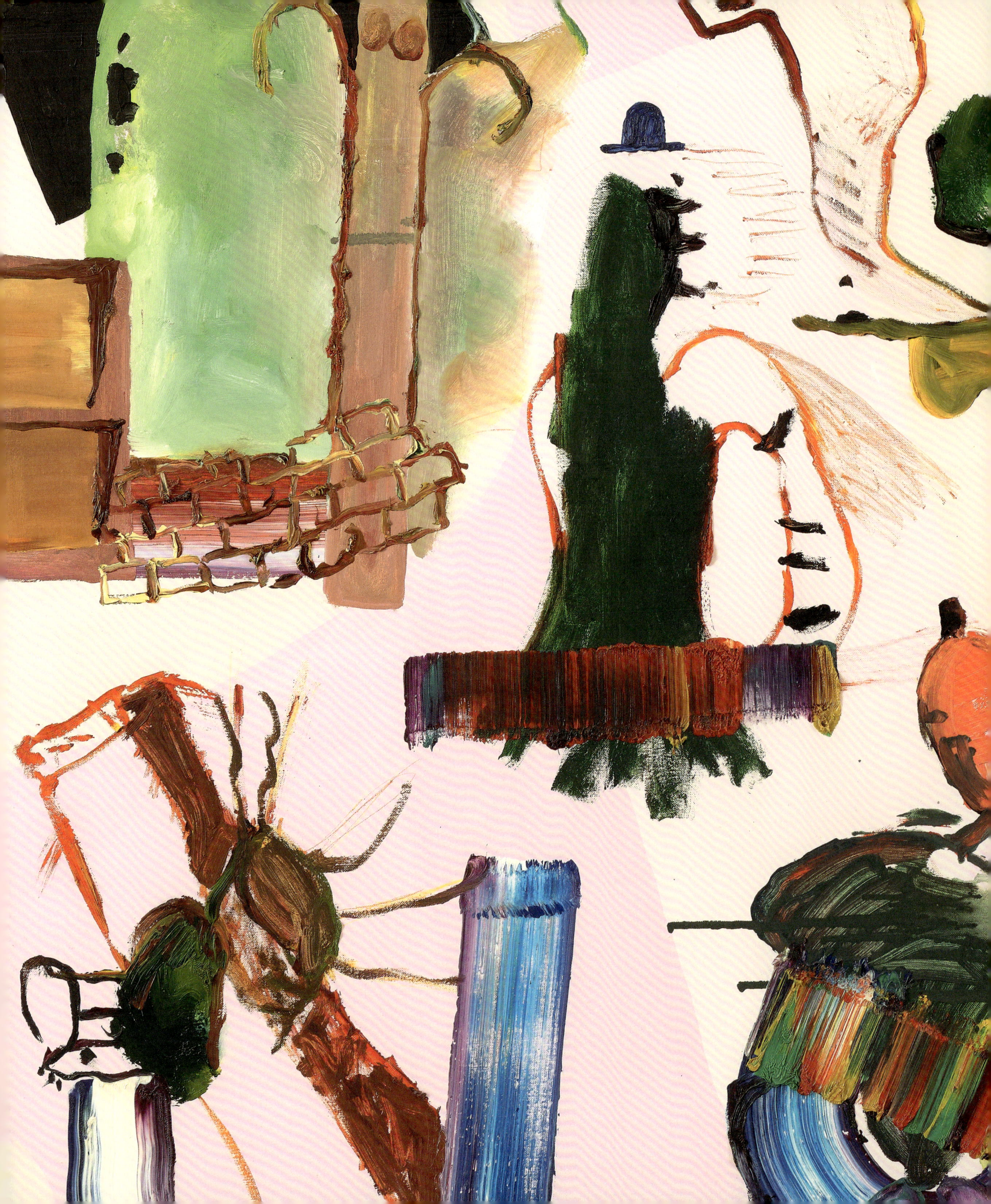

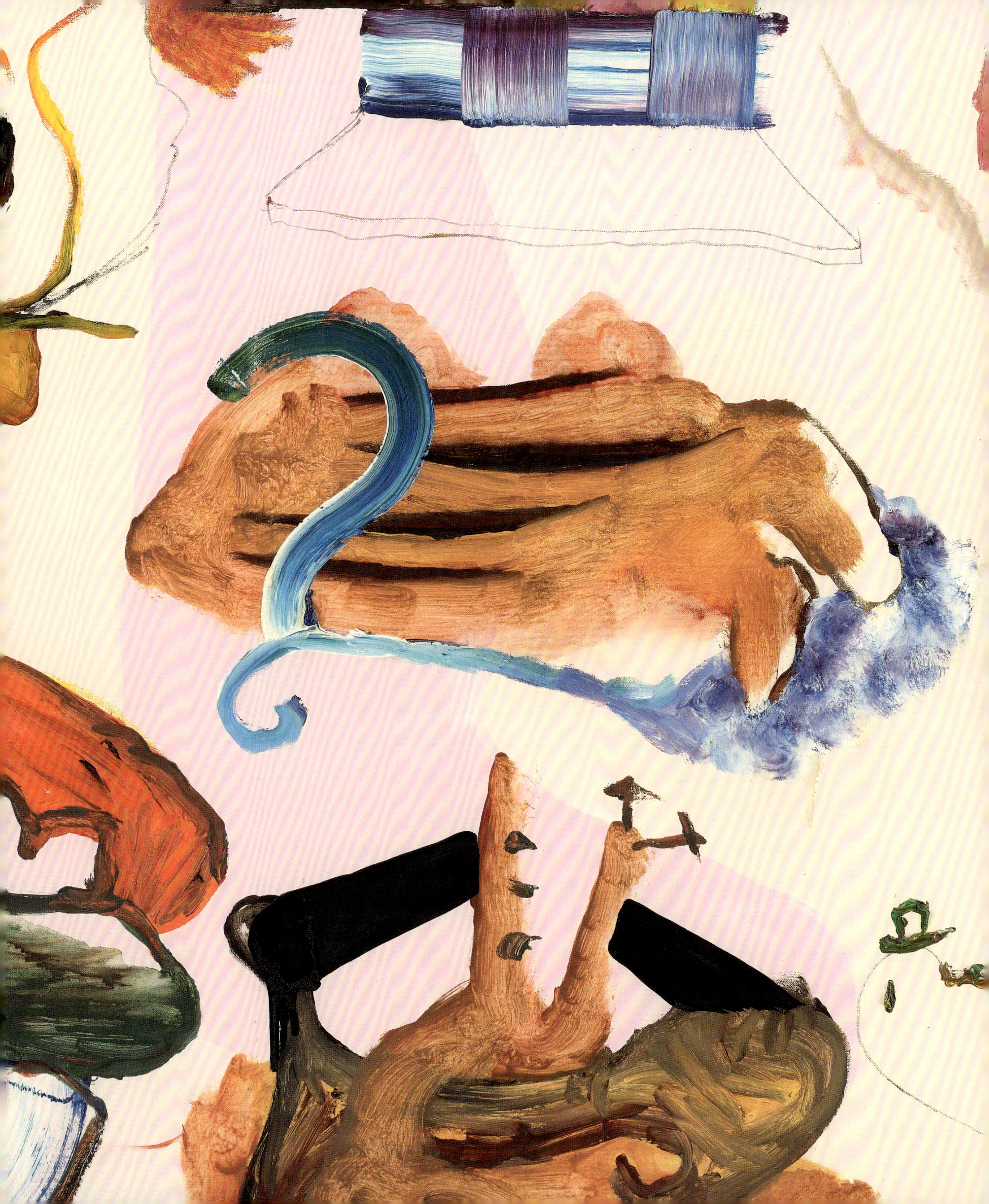

5
Untitled (five on pink), 1989
Oil and pencil on canvas
213.4 × 198.1 cm | 84 × 78 in

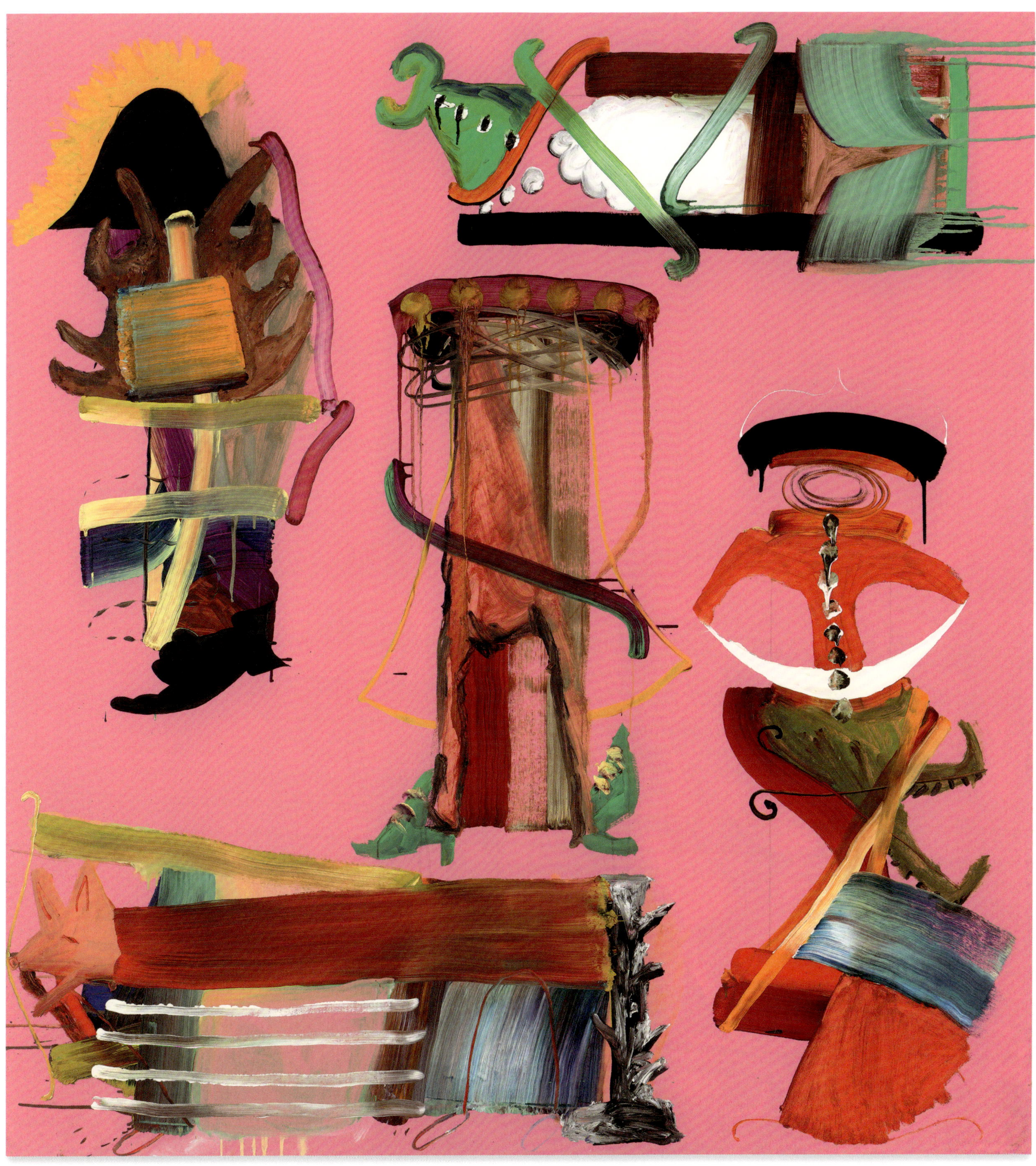

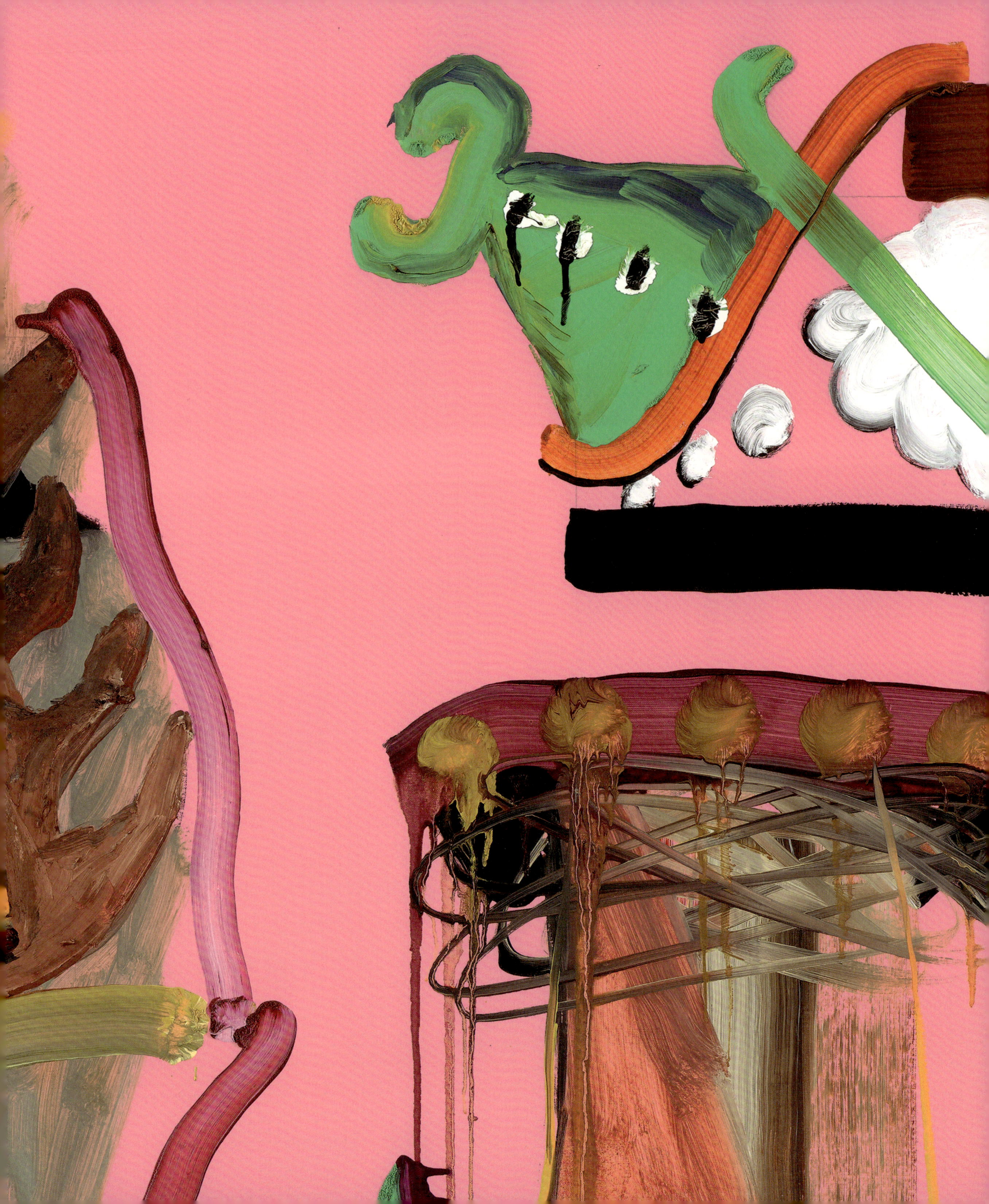

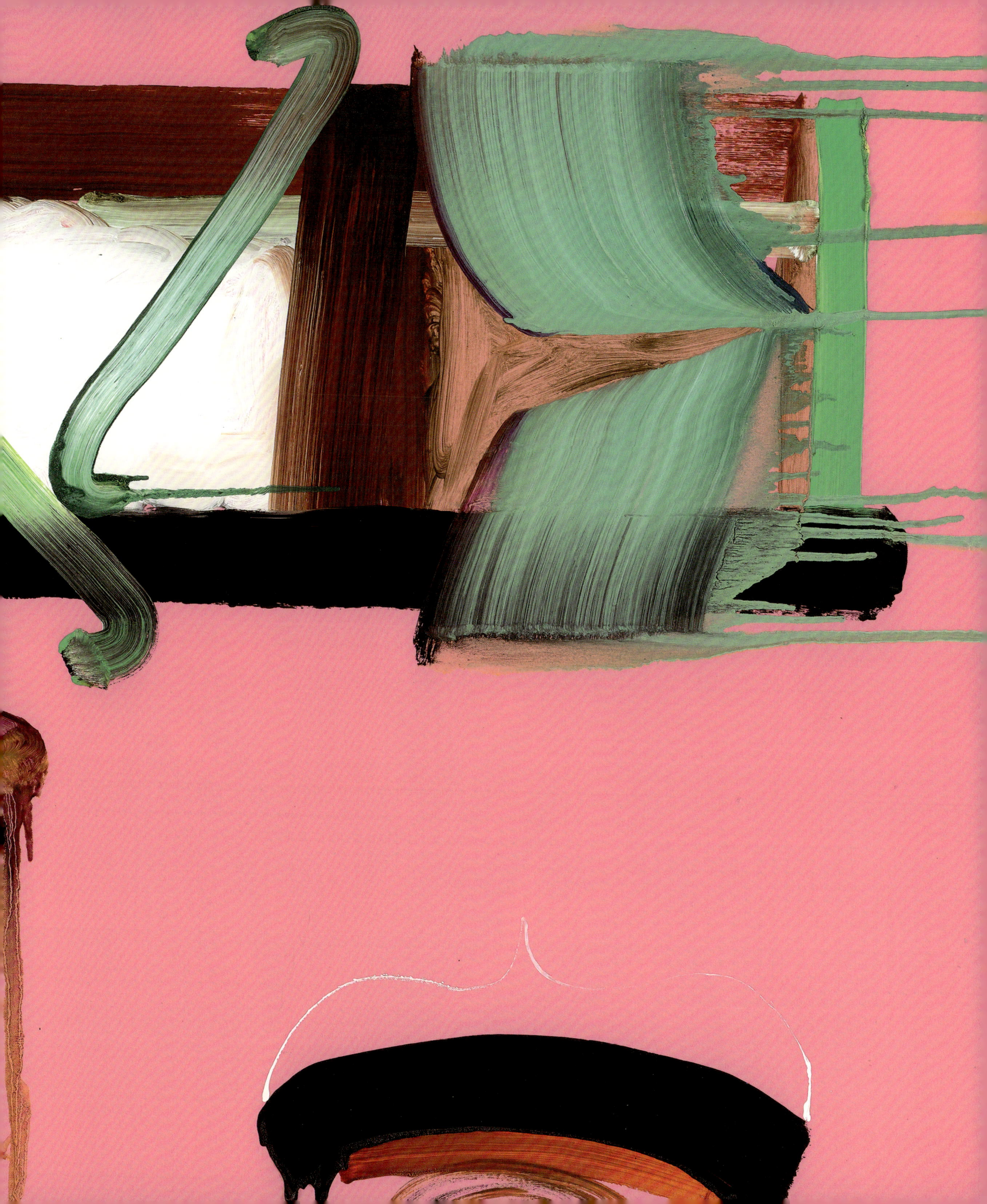

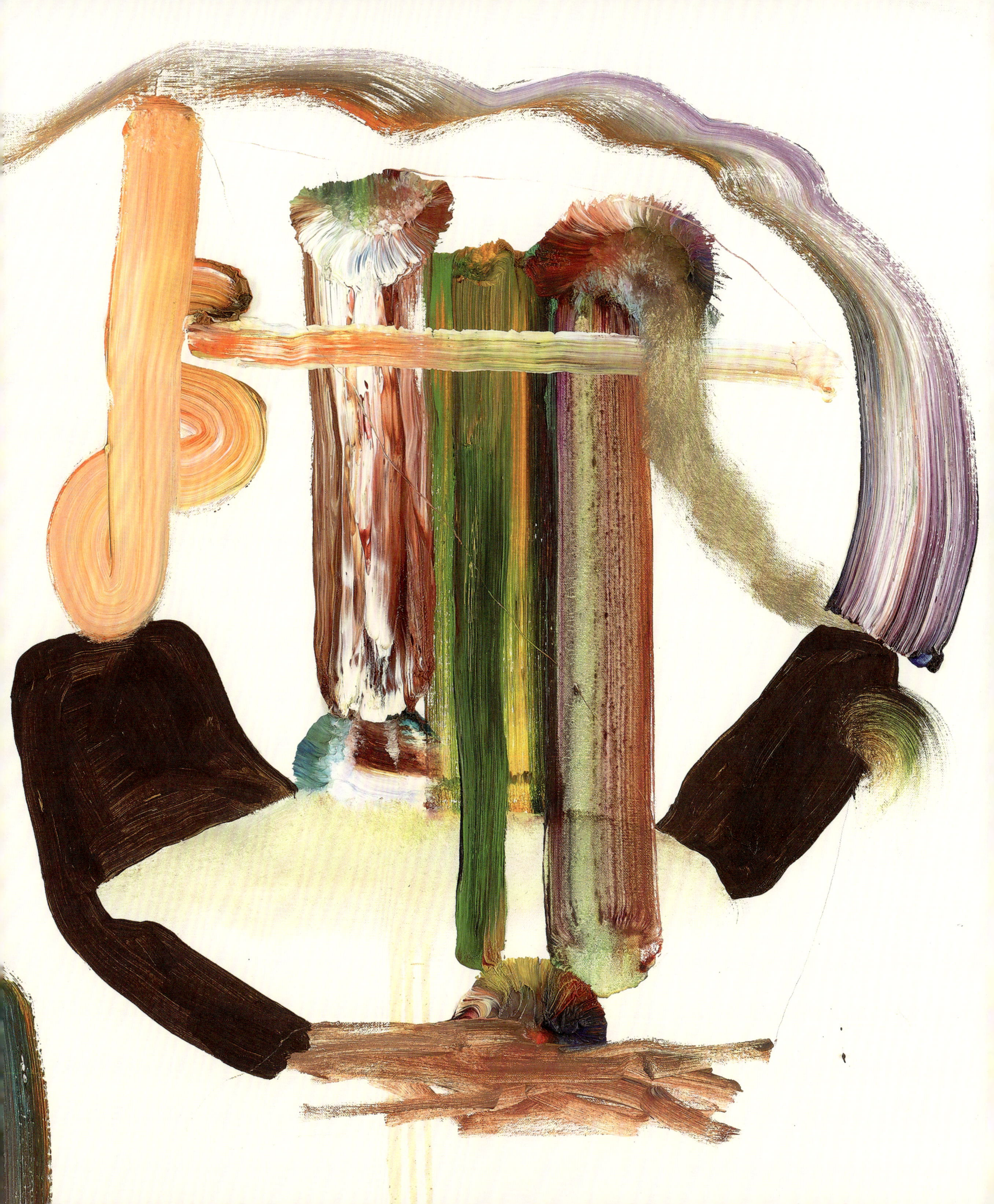

6

Untitled (nine on green), 1989
Oil on canvas
213.4 × 182.9 cm | 84 × 72 in

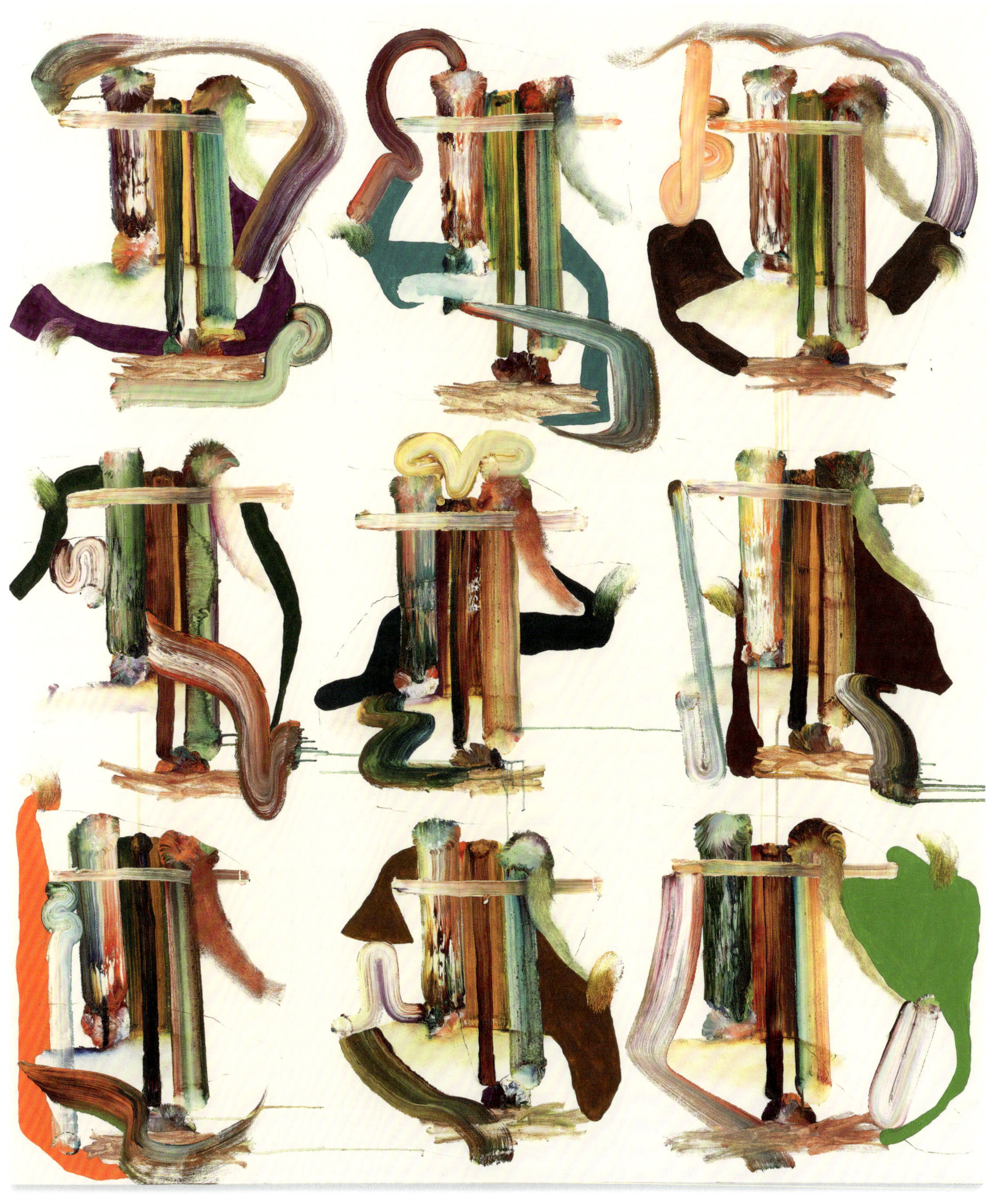

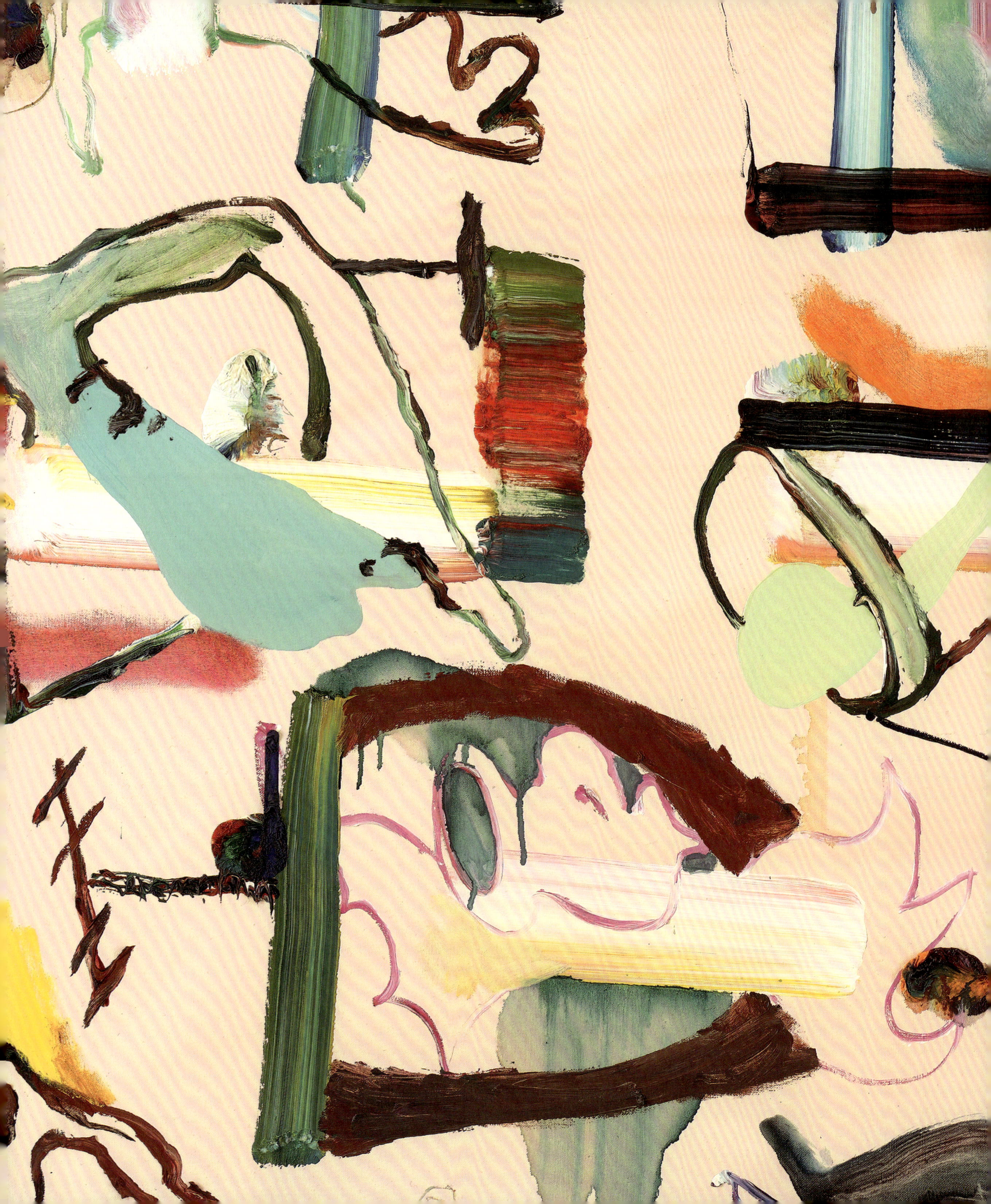

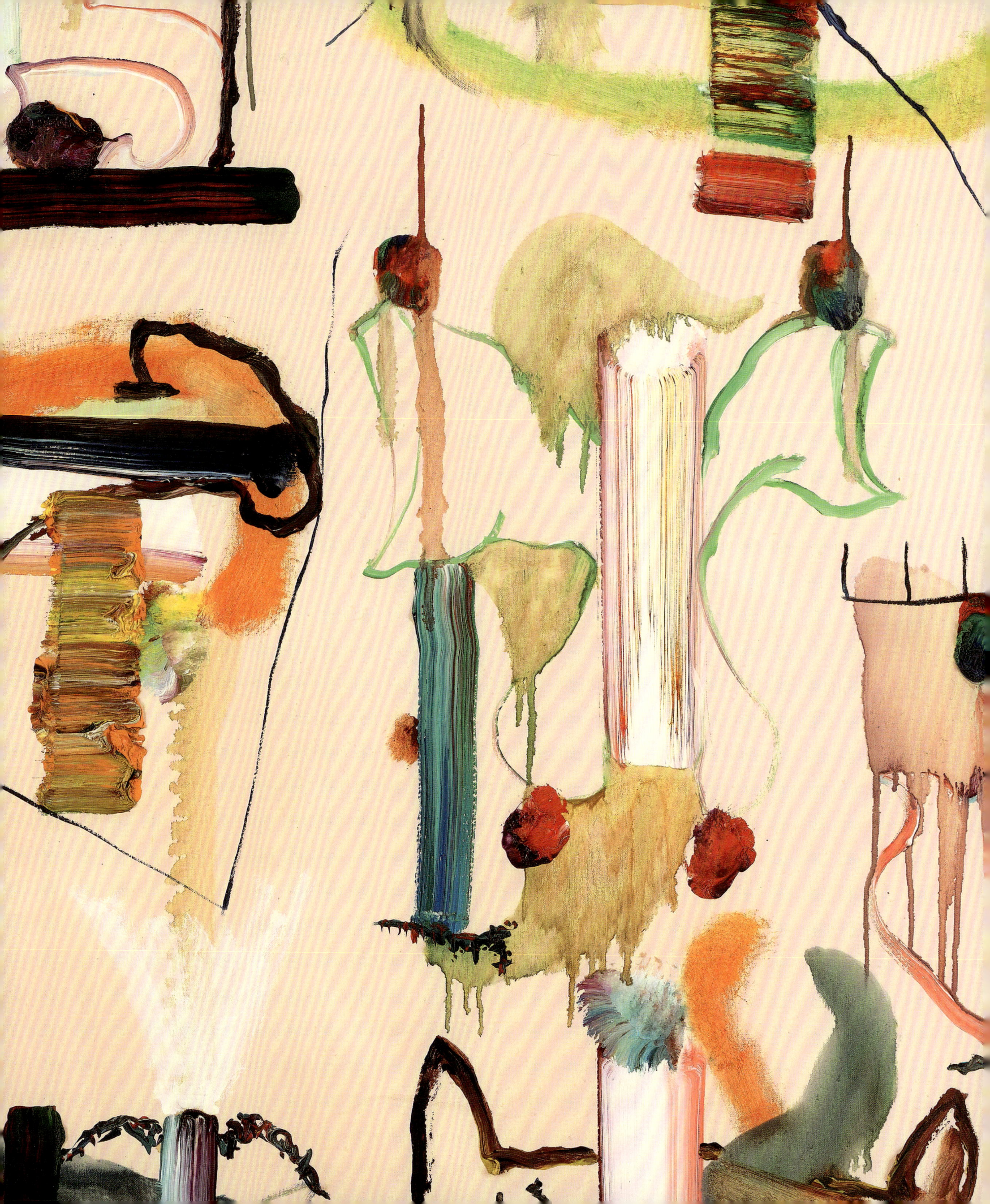

7
Untitled (twenty on orange), 1989
Oil on canvas
190.5 × 190.5 cm | 75 × 75 in

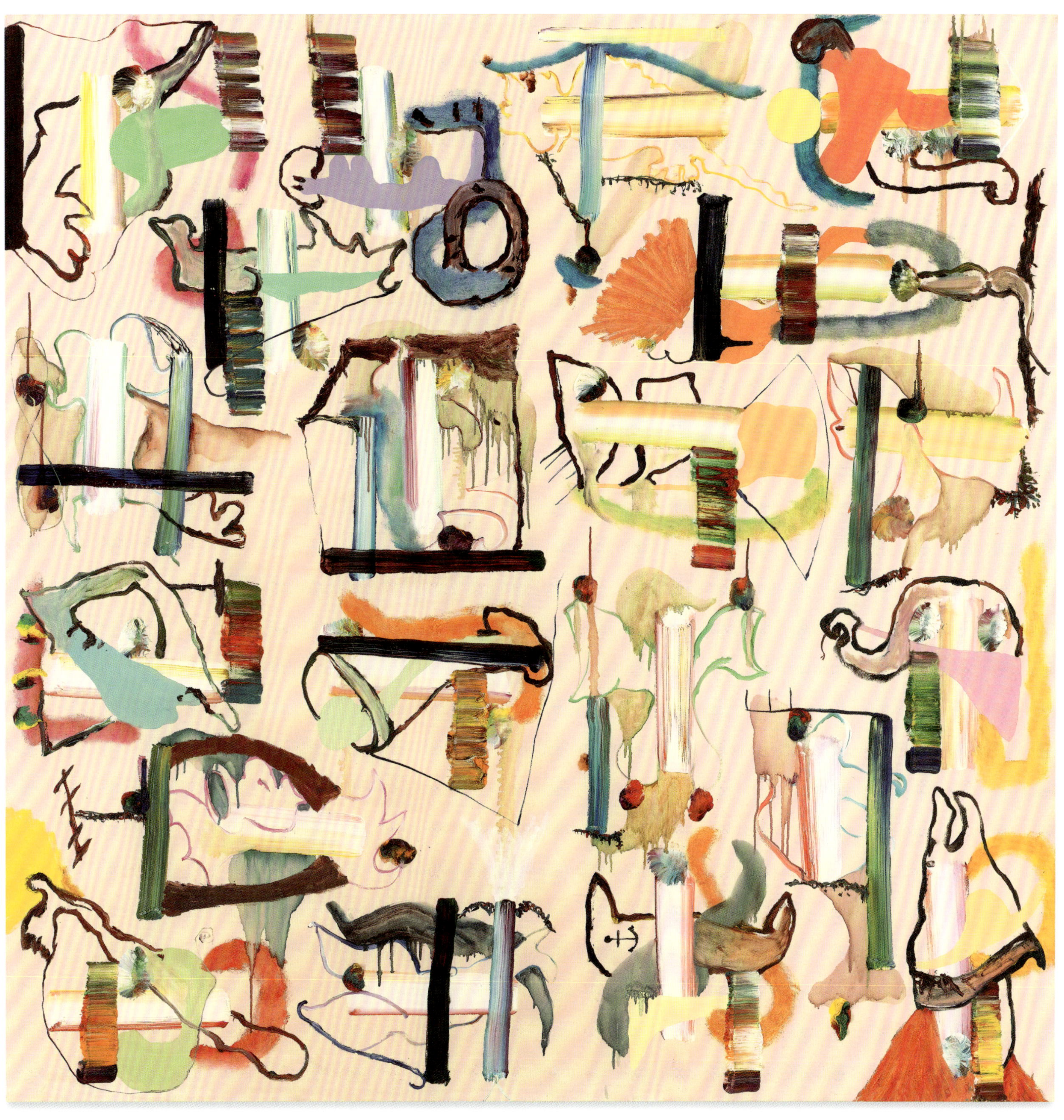

8

Untitled, 1988
Oil on canvas
182.9 × 167 cm | 72 × 65¾ in

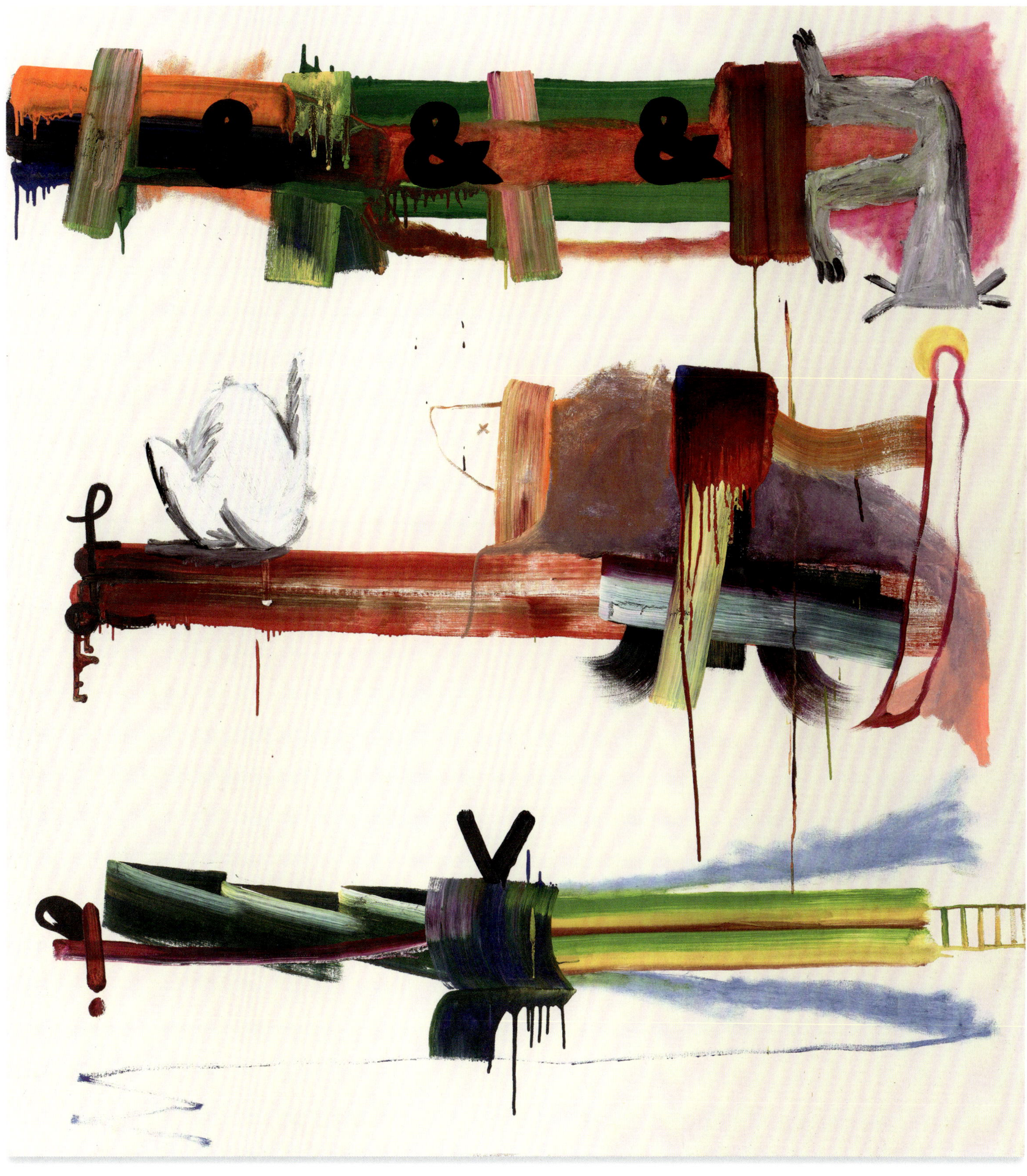

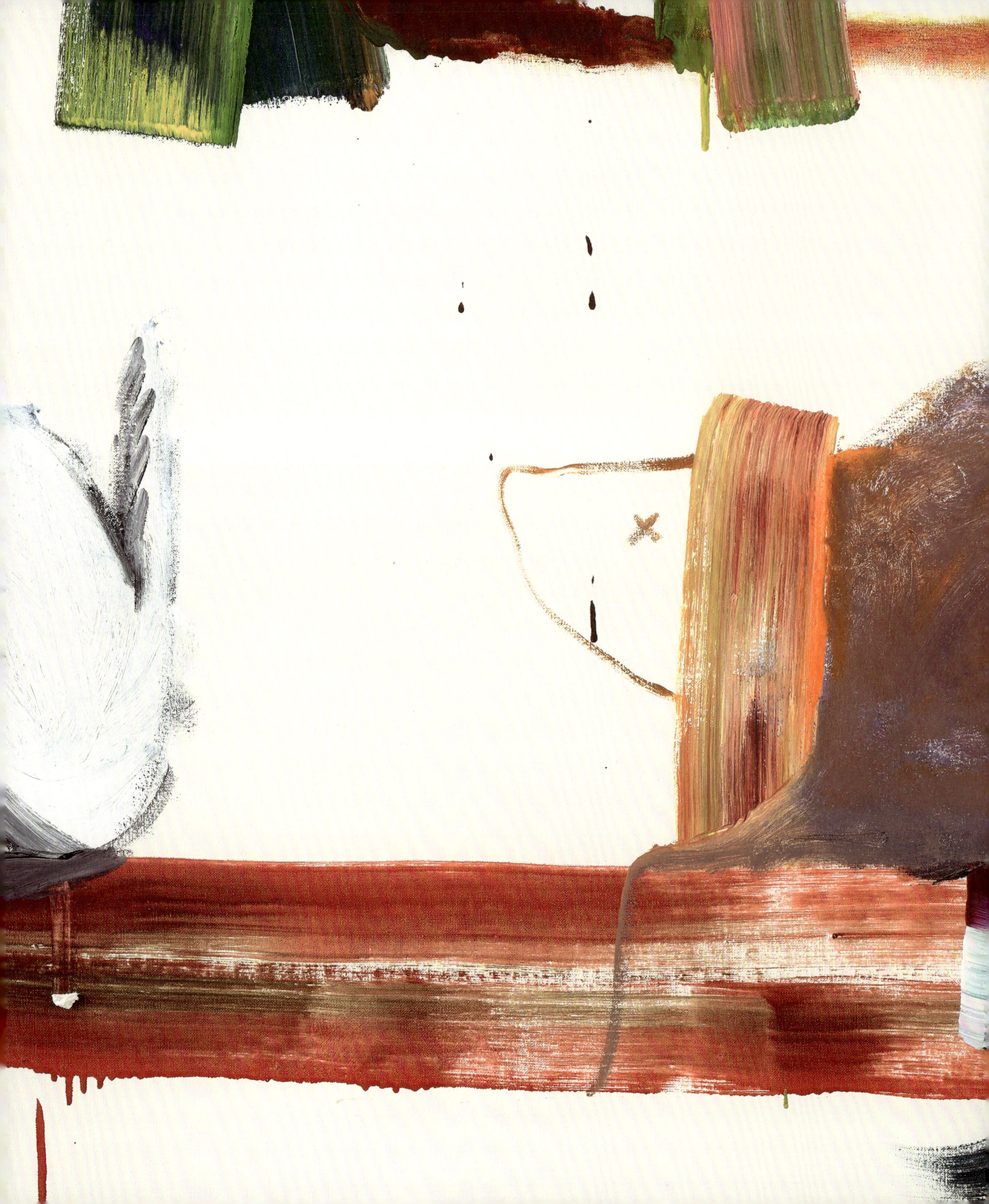

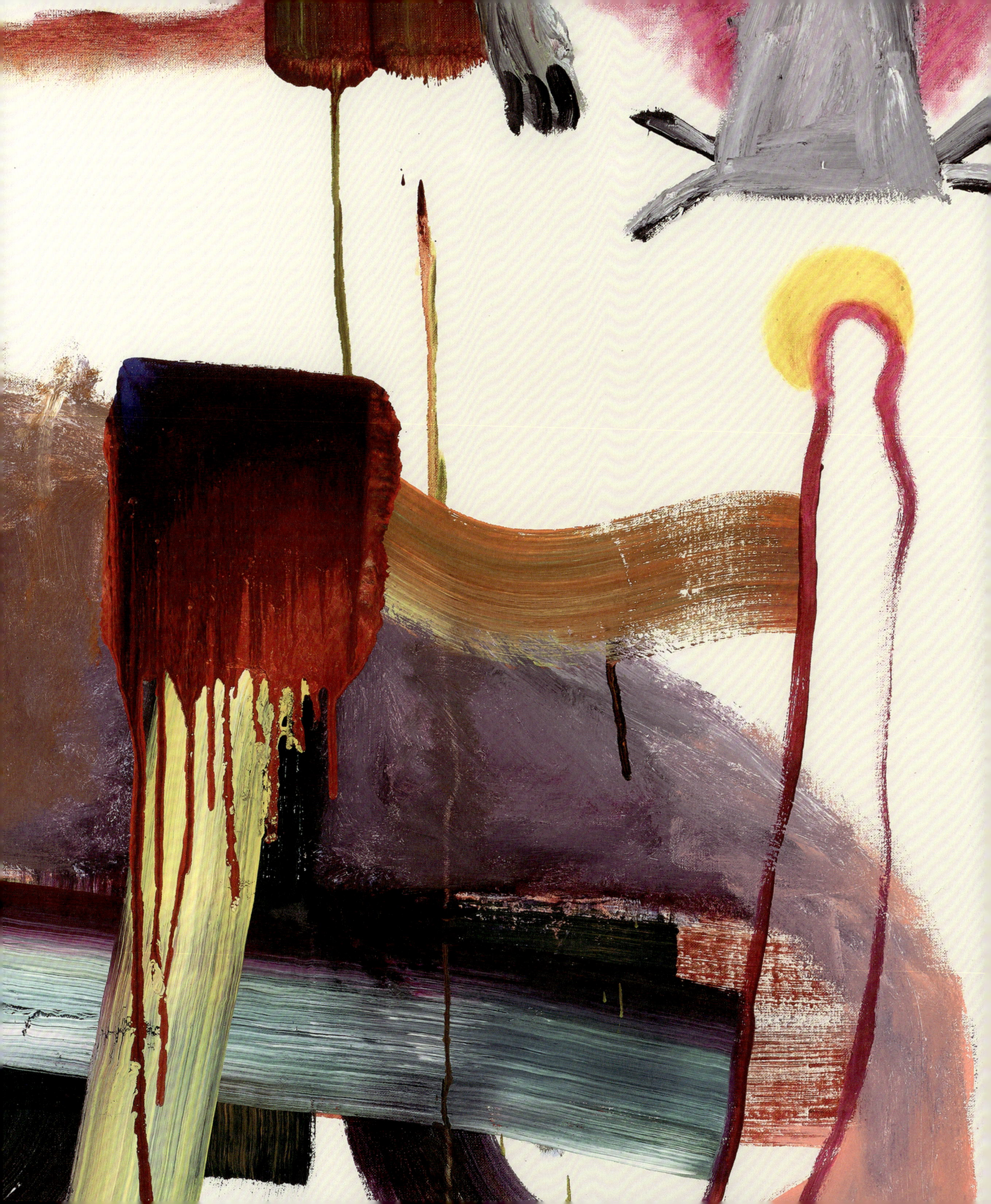

9
Untitled (nine on pale yellow), 1989
Oil and felt pen on canvas
152.4 × 152.4 cm | 60 × 60 in

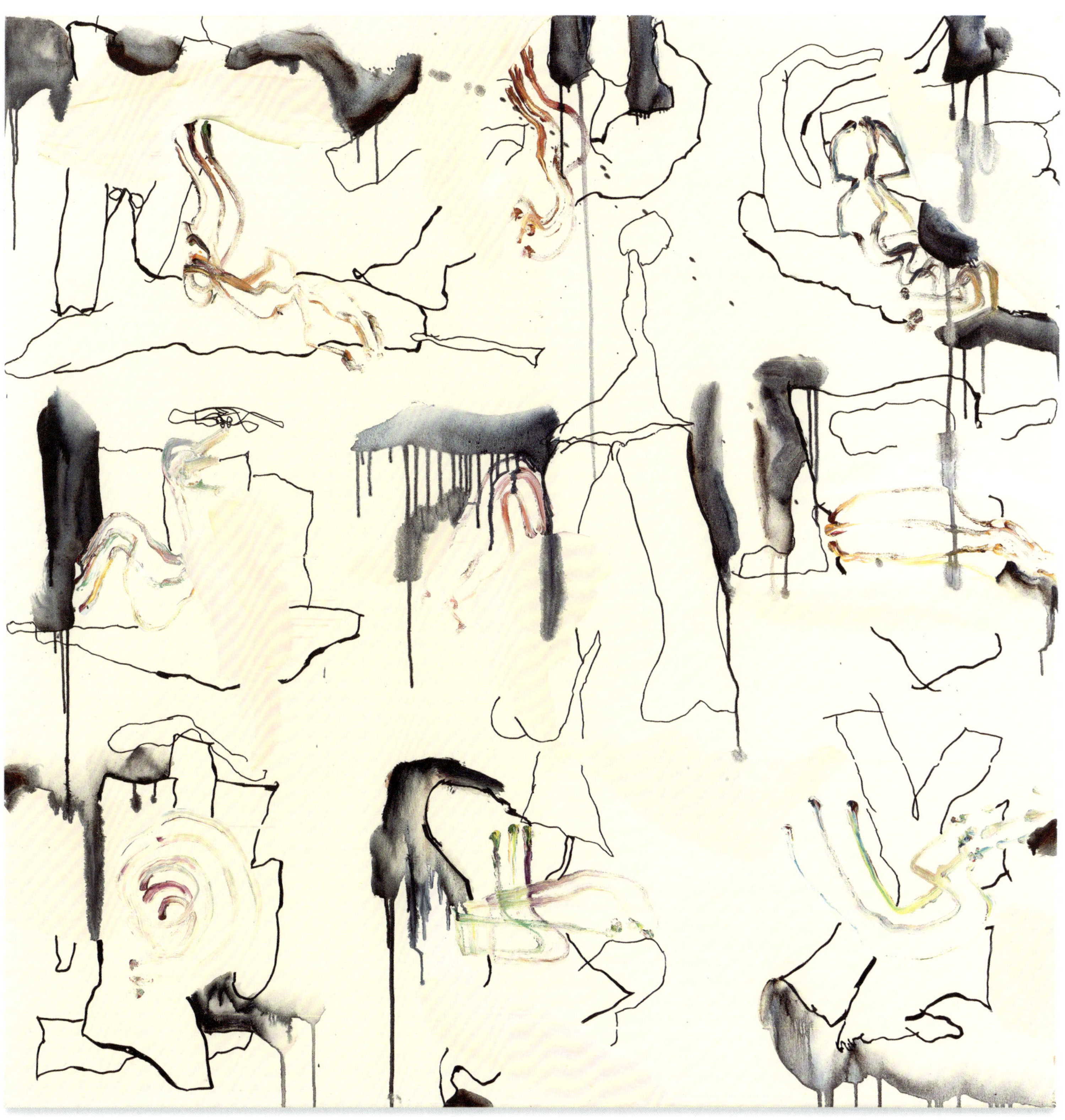

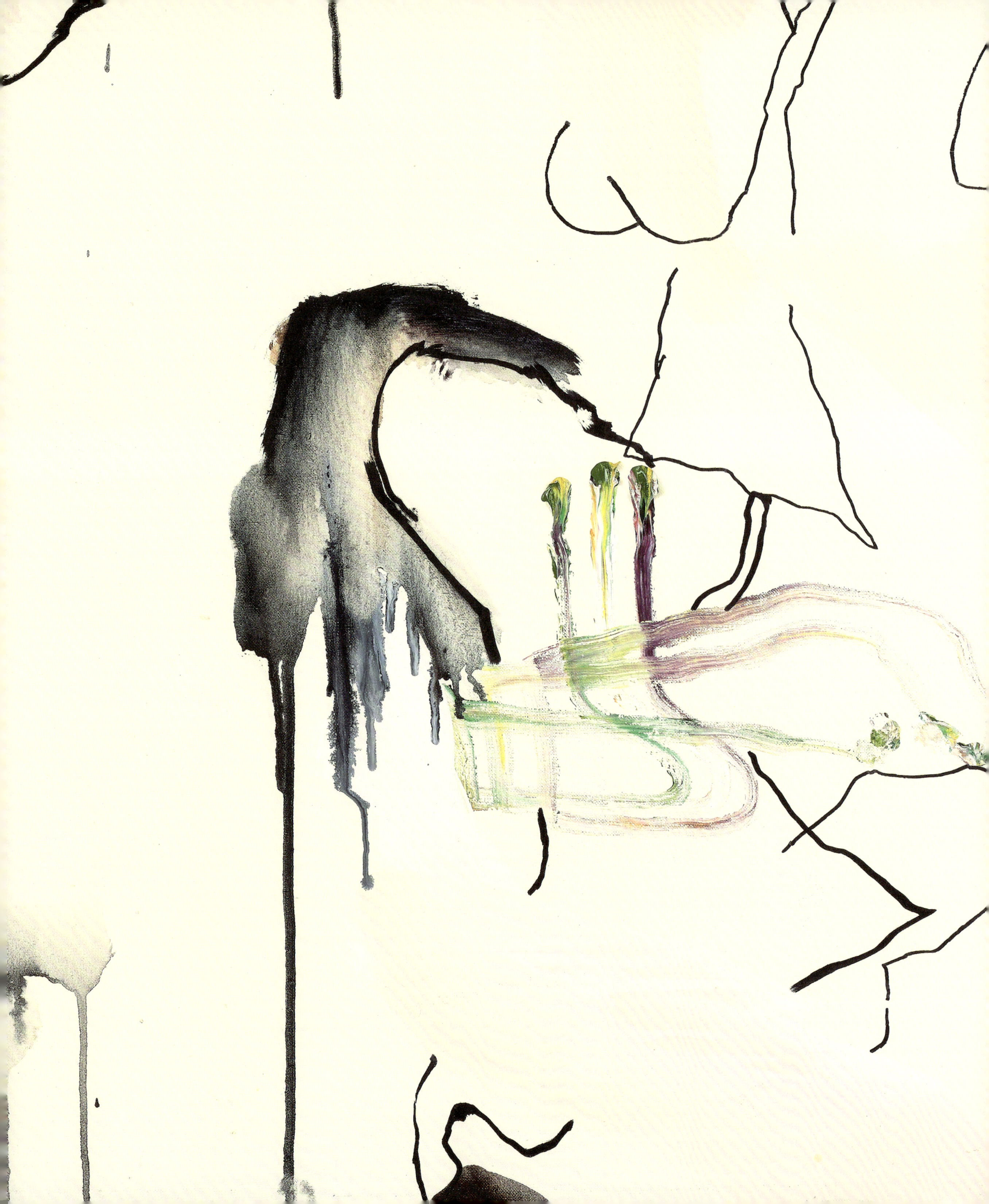

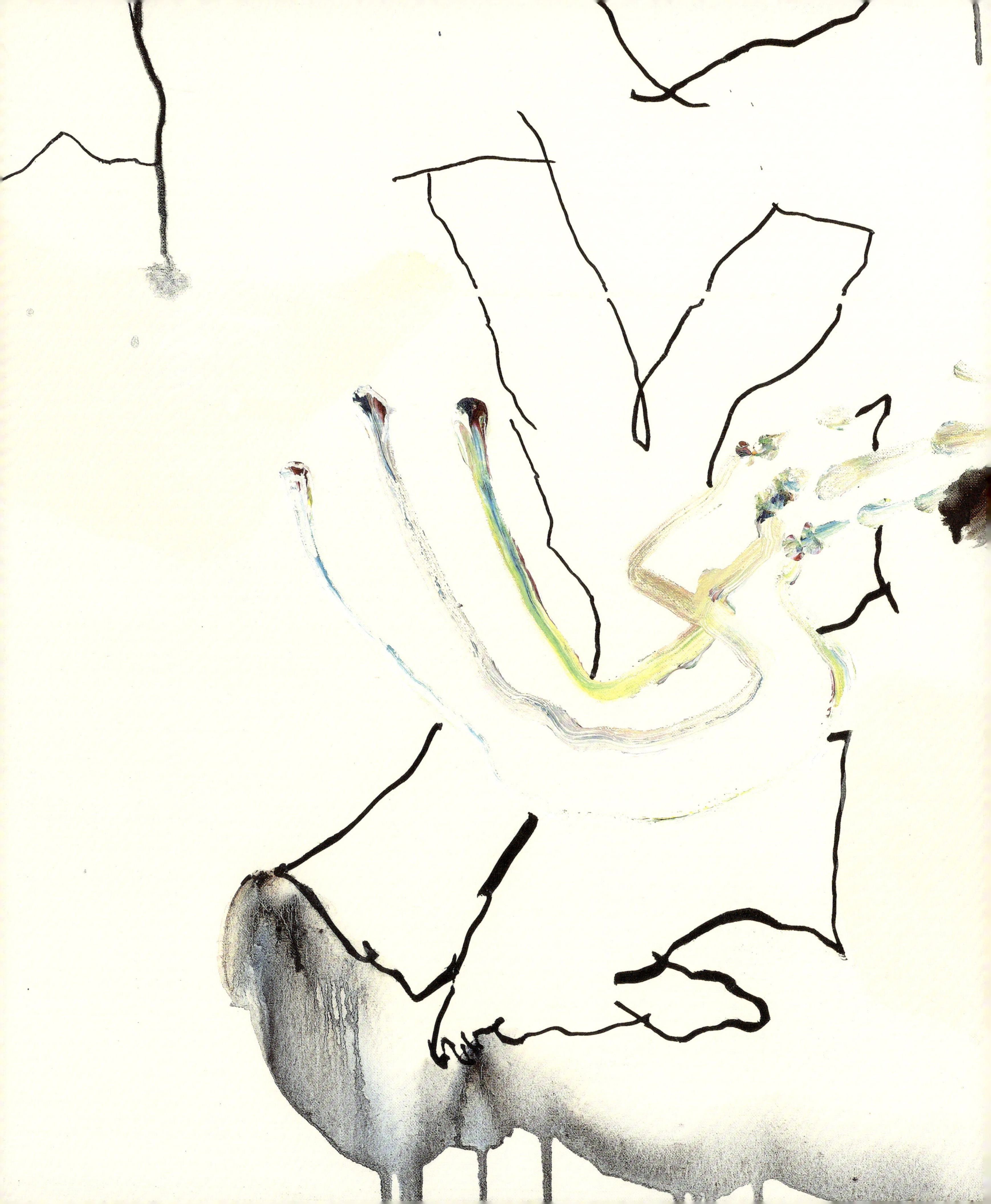

10

Untitled (one on green and grey), 1989
Oil on canvas
132.1 × 101.6 cm | 52 × 40 in

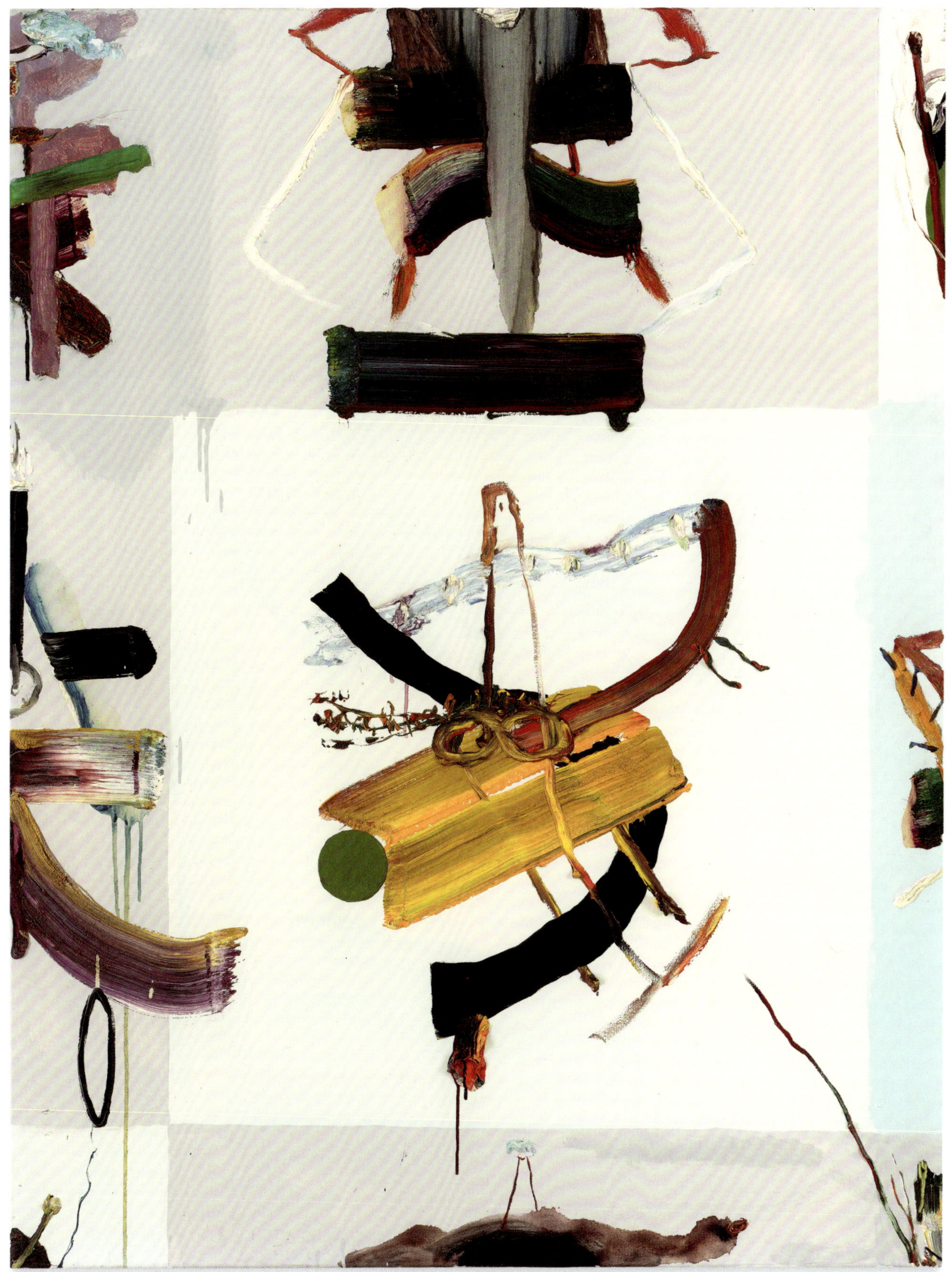

A Row is a Row is a Row

> *Und jetzt gilt das Interesse eher einer Balance, womit natürlich Wörter wie auch Dinge und Verteilungen gemeint sind sowohl untereinander unter Wörtern einander und Dingen einander, eine Verteilung als Verteilung. Das macht Kommendes zu Kommendem und nun gibt es gute Gründe dafür dass es ein Arrangement geben sollte. Verteilung ist interessant und Balance ist interessant wenn eine Verlaufsform der Gegenwart und ein wieder und wieder und wieder Beginnen und die Verwendung von allem da alles gleich und alles natürlich einfach anders ist schon dagewesen sind.*
>
> Gertrude Stein, „Komposition als Position"[1]

„Wörter wie auch Dinge und Verteilungen." Was kann man nach diesem Beispiel von Gertrude Steins perfektem – seiner Zeit weit vorauseilenden – rhetorischem und kritischen Ansinnen noch mehr über Fiona Raes auch ziemlich perfekte und vorausschauende *Row Paintings*, die sie in den späten 1980er-Jahren zu malen begann, sagen? Es stellt sich heraus, dass es noch viele, viele Dinge zu sagen gibt, weil es Gemälde sind, die zur Zeit ihrer Entstehung rege diskutiert wurden und diese kritischen Gespräche, die (wieder und wieder) über sie geführt wurden, in den dreißig und mehr Jahren ihrer Existenz nicht verstummt sind. Ich habe Raes Bilder zum ersten Mal 1994 in New York, zusammen mit anderen Gemälden gesehen, die mir nicht allein aufgrund der Qualität ihrer malerischen Energie und ihrer Farbgebung in Erinnerung geblieben sind, sondern auch aufgrund der Art, wie ihre Kompositionen funktionierten. Ich entsinne mich, dass diese besonderen Bilder Teil eines Diskurses über abstrakte Malerei waren, wie er seinerzeit in New York zudem über die Arbeiten von Lydia Dona, Shirley Kaneda, Jonathan Lasker und David Reed (die ich zum Glück alle persönlich kannte) in Umlauf war. Bemerkenswerter war allerdings der Bezug, die sie damals für mich zu den Arbeiten des Malers Lari Pittman aus Los Angeles hatten. Er und Rae brachten ein bisschen unterschiedlich etwas anderes aufs Tablett, das ich nicht verstand, bis ich diesen frühen Gemälden von Rae begegnete; ein Verstehen, das sich praktisch im selben Moment vollzog.

Wörter und Dinge und Verteilung *gerade jetzt*. In seinem Studio schlug Pittmann 1996 immer wieder mit der flachen Hand auf ein massives Gemälde ein, während er ausrief, dass „es einen Level von Insistenz erreicht hätte, wo alles sofort passiert!! Gerade, gerade, gerade jetzt!!" (Ich habe es auf Band aufgenommen und das Geräusch der Schläge überlagert alles.[2]) Vor ein paar Monaten hatten Rae und ich ein tiefgründiges Gespräch (virtuell via Zoom, und ich erwähne das deshalb, weil die aktuelle Krümmung von Zeit und Raum durch die Pandemie wunderbar zu meinen Argumenten passt), bei dem ich unmittelbar zurück in die Entstehungszeit ihrer Bilder katapultiert wurde.

Wie dem auch sei, diese Leinwände haben mehr als genug von dem, was sie brauchen, um in der immerwährenden Gegenwart zu existieren, welche die Malerei anscheinend oftmals ohne Anstrengung und Verzicht erreichen kann.

Es ist notwendig, zu erwähnen, dass Rae die *Row Paintings* 1988 auf der berühmten Ausstellung *Freeze* vorstellte, organisiert von ihrem Kommilitonen Damien Hirst während seines zweiten Studienjahrs am Goldsmiths. Auch wenn die Schau hinlänglich dafür bekannt ist, das absolut erfrischende Phänomen der Young British Artists ins Leben gerufen zu haben, finde ich es heute aufschlussreich, bis zu welchem Grad viele der hier gezeigten Arbeiten wie in Bernstein eingeschlossen erschienen, wie eingefroren, wenn man so will, in die Besonderheiten ihrer Zeit und ihres Ortes. Raes *Row Paintings* sind definitiv und voller Trotz entkommen, vor allem durch die Gleichzeitigkeit und Geschmeidigkeit der *Dreideutigkeit*, die sie formulieren und verkörpern.

Deshalb gilt bei diesen Gemälden: a row is a row is a row. Niemand, der sie betrachtet, muss darauf hingewiesen werden, dass sie ihre Formen in regelmäßigen Reihen auf der Leinwand präsentieren. Sie machen das ganz unapologetisch, fast als ob sie uns irgendwie beibringen wollten, nicht didaktisch mit ihnen umzugehen. (In anderen Worten, diese Bilder sind alles, außer mathematische Aufgaben, die gelöst werden müssen.) *Untitled (nine on green)* (Tfl. 6) zum Beispiel kann als das unkomplizierteste Bild der Serie angesehen werden: drei Reihen mit je drei exzentrischen Formen, die an einem tragenden grünlichen Gerüst aufgehängt sind. Die neun Formen sind ähnlich, aber nicht identisch: Rae zufolge wurden sie Stück für Stück gemalt, indem sie sich von Form zu Form vorarbeitete und denselben Pinselstrich für jede benutzte, dann von Neuem mit einem anderen Strich begann und mit ihrer Runde so lange fortfuhr, bis das Gemälde komplett fertig war.[3] Rae verwandte auch sehr viel Arbeit darauf, ihre Pinsel zu verändern. So schraubte sie beispielsweise zwei zusammen, um ein unhandliches Gerät daraus zu machen, oder sie erhitzte sie in Hasenleim, was diese ziemlich ruinierte. Ich glaube, derartige Aktionen verstärken den Eindruck, den ich von Raes Werk schon immer gehabt und bis heute habe. Wie viele der bedeutendsten Maler, jedenfalls seit Francis Picabia, beschäftigt sie sich (und noch wichtiger, spielt sie) mit den fundamentalen Widersprüchen der Malerei und bezieht keine Stellung. (Sie erzählte mir, während wir über Robert Rauschenbergs *Erased de Kooning Drawing* von 1953 sprachen, dass sie immer de Kooning und Rauschenberg gleichzeitig sein wollte.)

Diese beiden Künstler teilen, wie ihr spiritueller und konzeptueller Pate Marcel Duchamp, eine Hingabe an die verbale Sprache und ihre geschriebene Form. De Kooning begann Gemälde oft mit schnell auf die Leinwand skizzierten Buchstaben (in manchen seiner vollendeten Bilder sind sie noch lesbar), und Rauschenberg brachte Text direkt auf das „schwarze Brett" seiner Oberflächen auf ebenso wie durch den Gebrauch der bildlichen Versionen von Wortspielen wie dem Rebus. Alle *Row Paintings* von Rae sind eine Präsentation von einzelnen Buchstaben, keine von Wörtern oder Sätzen, aber – wie ich es eben über de Koonings Bilder von 1956 bis 1959 geschrieben habe – „jedes funktioniert gleichzeitig als Gemälde und als Übertragung der Malerei an sich".[4] Dies bestätigt die kraftvolle Reihe ihrer Bilder, weil sie sich selbst als Argumente für und gegen Malerei, aber auch als Erweiterung der gemalten Pinselstriche jenseits von Kategorien wie Abstraktion, Figuration, schön und hässlich erweisen. Das hier sind kämpferische Gemälde, die nicht nur lautstark gegen das kurzsichtige Gerede vom Ende der Malerei in den späten 1980er- und frühen 1990er-Jahren aufbegehren, sondern auch – sagen wir – sich sehr darin gefallen, sich miteinander zu streiten.

Es mag jetzt nicht allzu sehr überraschen, dass Rae am Goldsmiths nicht besonders vertraut mit den Bildern der oben erwähnten New Yorker Malerinnen und Maler war, sich aber gut mit den durch Texte und Grafikdesign inspirierten Arbeiten der 1980er Jahre von Jenny Holzer und Barbara Kruger auskannte. (Rae hatte auch englische Literatur studiert, bevor sie zur bildenden Kunst wechselte.) Dies zu wissen hilft die der kompositorischen Klarheit zugrunde liegende Komplexität der *Row Paintings*, ebenso wie die schon fast programmatische Verteilung ihrer gemeinsamen Begriffe von Gemälde zu Gemälde verstehen zu können. Eines der ersten mit dem einfachen Titel *Untitled* (Tfl. 8), trennt und stapelt drei abstrakte horizontale „Sichtachsen", als ob sie in der Auslage eines Schaufensters lägen oder auf einer Bühne auftreten würden. Mehr noch, keine der Ansichten versucht, die Vielfalt ihrer Komponenten zu verbergen: kaufmännische Und-Zeichen und das Symbol für das britische Pfund raufen sich mit pelzigen Kreaturen und Leitern (oder Zugschienen, oder, bei anderen Bildern, direkten Anspielungen auf das Werk von einflussreichen Künstlern wie etwa Philip Guston), da sie auf Farbfeld-ähnlichen, gemalten, bunten Bändern in verschiedenen Ausführungen platziert wurden. *Untitled (fourteen on green and pink)* (Tfl. 1) hat eine um 45 Grad nach rechts (Osten?) gedrehte Komposition und seine 14 gemalten Formen gleichen noch mehr irgendwelchen Lebewesen. Malerei, erscheint jetzt mit der Karikatur-Ausgabe von Malerei zusammen (Rae erzählte mir von ihrer einschneidenden Entdeckung des Werks von George Herriman als Studentin), verteilt auf so etwas wie Steins Balance, die die „Verlaufsform der Gegenwart" hervorbringen kann, von der sie so klar komplex spricht, oder vice versa.

Die letzte Reihe ist eher wie die erste. Und im Sinne von Sprache ist es wahrscheinlich die größte Herausforderung, aber das ist für mich der springende Punkt. Die Elastizität ist am wichtigsten. Row (Reihe) als Verb (to row, rudern), beschreibt die Schläge, die man im Wasser macht, um sich selbst von einem Punkt zum anderen voranzutreiben. Die Zeitspanne von Raes *Row Paintings* unterscheidet sich nicht allzu sehr von einer Fahrt in einem Ruderboot den Fluss hinunter, auch wenn sie in der Lage wären, sich auch selbst mithilfe eines Rotorblatts oder einer Rakete fortzubewegen. Der visuelle Beweis (Überrest) der Pinselschläge, die gemacht wurden, um diese Gemälde zu bewegen, bestätigt erneut, dass sie dann inszeniert wurden, als die Farbe noch flüssig war oder zumindest etwas formbarer als das, was sie später wurden. Rae verdoppelt diesen Effekt mit expliziten Hinweisen darauf, dass viele der Bilder an den Seiten geneigt sind, damit die Farbe in jede Richtung laufen konnte, auch in die, die in visueller Hinsicht der Schwerkraft entgegenwirkt. (So zum Beispiel *Untitled (six on grey 1)* [Tfl. 2].) Das ist die Reihe, die uns, hier am Ende, gerade rechtzeitig, erlöst. Während unseres Gesprächs erwähnte Rae einen früheren Aufsatz von mir über die Arbeit des Quantengravitationsphysikers Carlo Rovelli, insbesondere seine Aussage, ein Gestein sei ein sehr langsames Ereignis.[5] Gemälde sind dann also Dinge, die einem Wimpernschlag viel, viel näher sind (was die Frage nach sich zieht, was wir selbst sind), aber die Fähigkeit haben, diesen Augenblick gerade jetzt festzuhalten, gerade, gerade, gerade jetzt. Und das wird ganz sicher immer den einzigartigen Wert aufzeigen, manchmal vor ihnen stehenzubleiben.

Terry R. Myers

ANMERKUNGEN

1. Gertrude Stein, „Komposition als Position", erstmals publiziert 1926, zit. nach: Uda Strätling (Hg.), *Gertrude Stein – Das große Lesebuch*, Frankfurt am Main 2017, S. 264.
2. „Lari Pittman In Conversation with Terry R. Myers", erstmals publiziert 1996, wie exzerpiert in: Terry R. Myers (Hg.), *Painting (Documents of Contemporary Art)*, London und Cambridge, MA, 2011, S. 117f.
3. Mein Gespräch mit der Künstlerin fand am 27. März 2021 via Zoom statt.
4. Siehe mein „Make Way for de Kooning", in: *The Brooklyn Rail*, Oktober 2011, unter https://brooklynrail.org/2011/10/artseen/make-way-for-de-kooning (zuletzt aufgerufen am 30. Mai 2021).
5. Siehe Carlo Rovelli, *The Order of Time*, New York, 2018 und meinen Essay „Katharina Grosse: I See What She Did There", in: *Gagosian Quarterly*, Sommer 2020, unter https://gagosian.com/quarterly/2020/04/21/katharina-grosse-i-see-what-she-did-there/ (zuletzt aufgerufen am 30. Mai 2021).

Terry R. Myers lebt als Autor und Kurator in Los Angeles und ist Editor-at-Large bei *The Brooklyn Rail*. Er ist der Verfasser von *Mary Heilmann: Save the Last Dance for Me* (2007) und der Herausgeber von *Painting: Documents of Contemporary Art* (2011). Sein jüngstes kuratorisches Projekt war die große Einzelausstellung *Candida Alvarez: Here* im Chicago Cultural Center im Jahr 2017. Von 2013 bis 2018 war er Leiter des Fachbereichs Malerei und Zeichnung an der School of the Art Institute of Chicago.

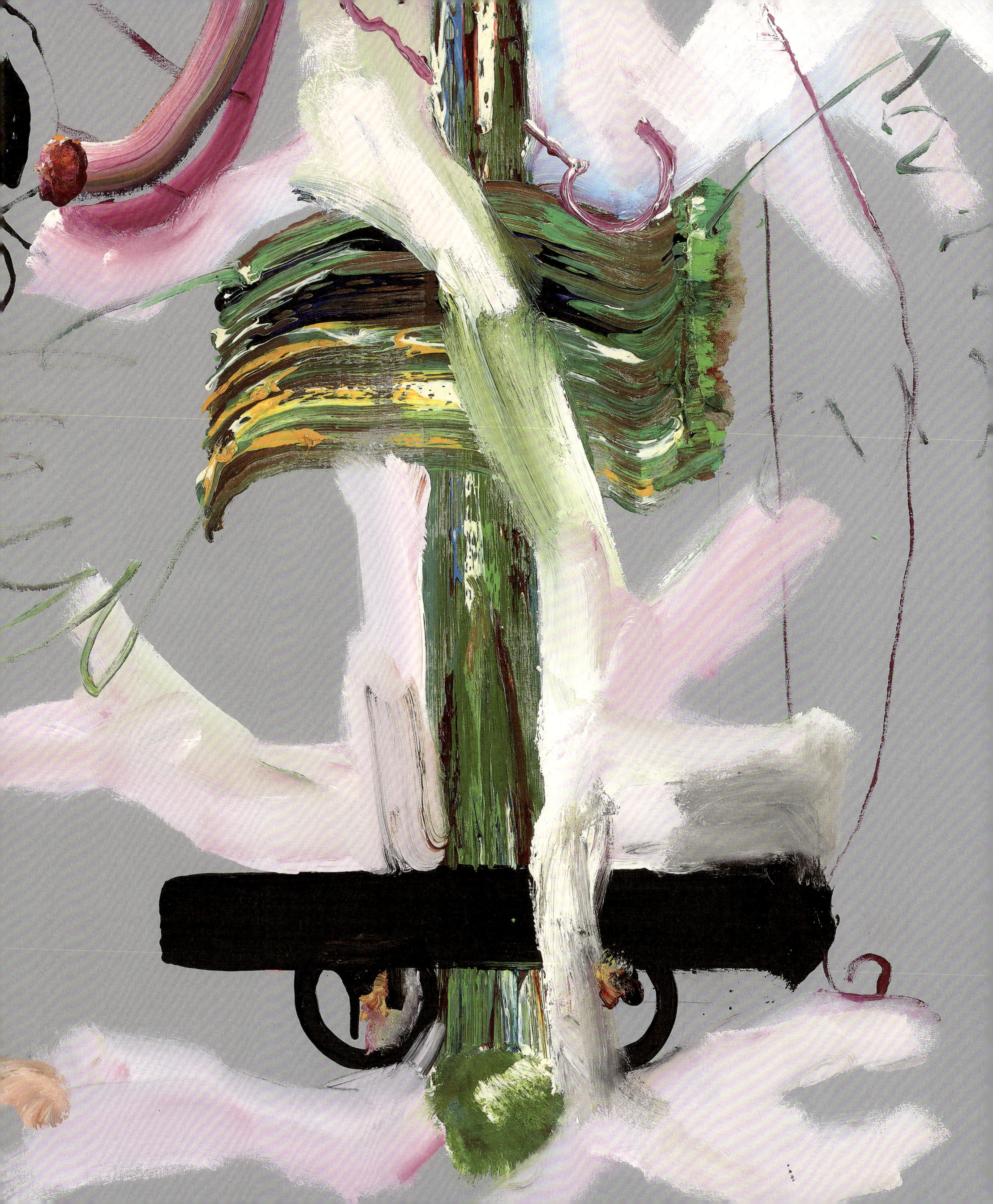

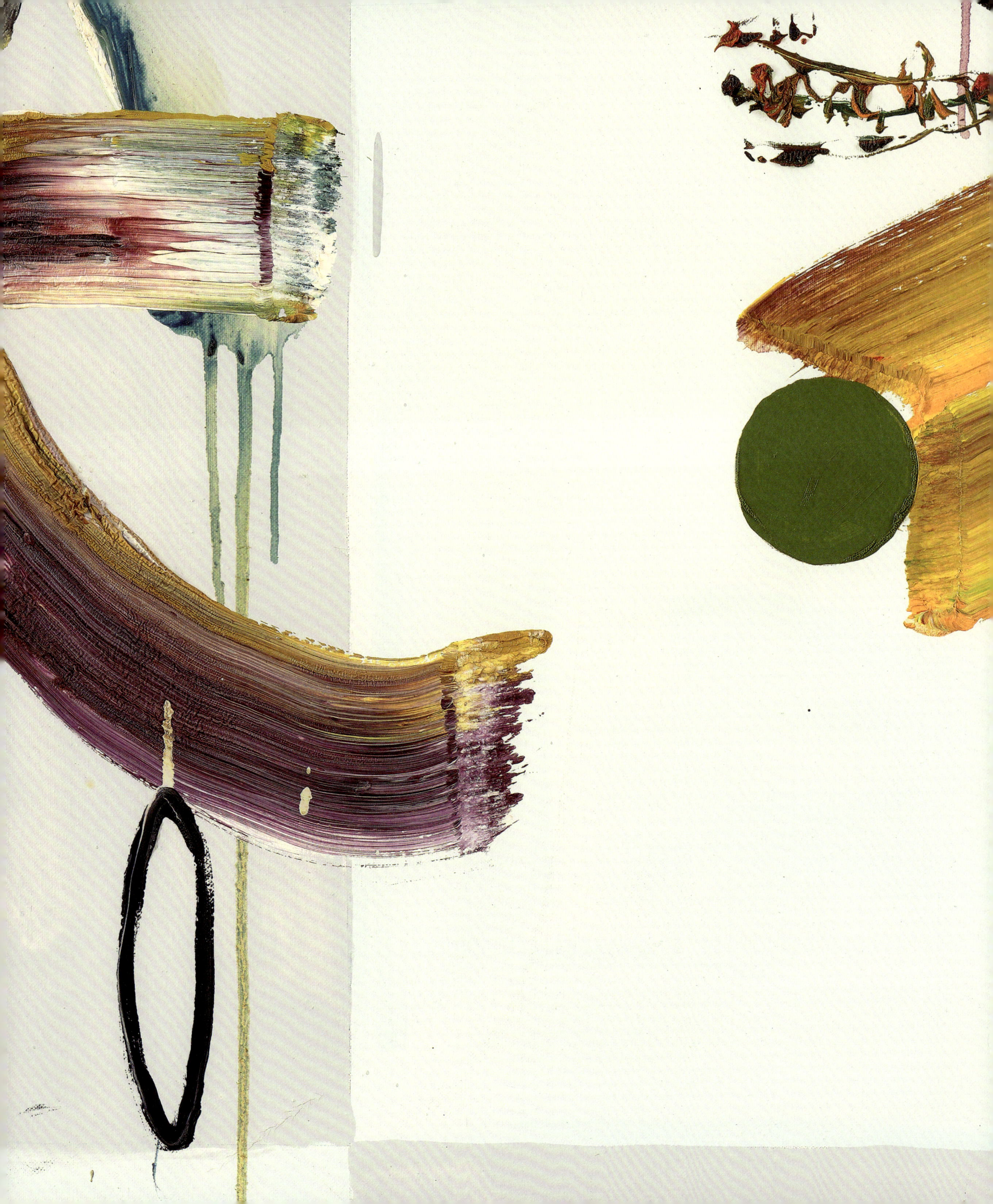

List of Works | Werkliste

1
Untitled (fourteen on green and pink)
1989
Oil and felt pen on canvas
Öl und Filzstift auf Leinwand
127 × 109.2 cm | 50 × 43 in

2
Untitled (six on grey 1)
1990
Oil on canvas
Öl auf Leinwand
213.4 × 198.1 cm | 84 × 78 in

3
Untitled (six on pink and yellow)
1989
Oil on canvas
Öl auf Leinwand
213.4 × 198.1 cm | 84 × 78 in

4
Untitled (twenty on two pinks and yellow)
1989
Oil and pencil on canvas
Öl und Bleistift auf Leinwand
213.4 × 198.1 cm | 84 × 78 in

5
Untitled (five on pink)
1989
Oil and pencil on canvas
Öl und Bleistift auf Leinwand
213.4 × 198.1 cm | 84 × 78 in

6
Untitled (nine on green)
1989
Oil on canvas
Öl auf Leinwand
213.4 × 182.9 cm | 84 × 72 in

7
Untitled (twenty on orange)
1989
Oil on canvas
Öl auf Leinwand
190.5 × 190.5 cm | 75 × 75 in

8
Untitled
1988
Oil on canvas
Öl auf Leinwand
182.9 × 167 cm | 72 × 65¾ in

9
Untitled (nine on pale yellow)
1989
Oil and felt pen on canvas
Öl und Filzstift auf Leinwand
152.4 × 152.4 cm | 60 × 60 in

10
Untitled (one on green and grey)
1989
Oil on canvas
Öl auf Leinwand
132.1 × 101.6 cm | 52 × 40 in

Biography

Over the last thirty years Fiona Rae has produced a distinctive body of work rooted in a conceptual examination of the problems and possibilities of abstract painting. Rae frequently reinvigorates her practice through self-imposed strategic challenges, which have resulted in over fifteen different series of paintings to date. The paintings are improvised directly onto the canvas, establishing painterly and semiotic codes within which each visual element has an equal importance and significance in an inclusive and democratic fictive space. Known for their iconoclastic approach to subject matter and formal concerns, Fiona Rae's paintings incarnate an abstract-pop universe, filled with references to modern and contemporary painting, pop culture, and digital technology.

Fiona Rae was born in Hong Kong in 1963. After studying at Croydon College of Art and Goldsmiths College in London, Rae took part in the groundbreaking exhibition *Freeze* in London's Docklands in 1988, becoming one of the first representatives of the Young British Artists (YBAs) who were to change the British art world and beyond.

In 1991, Fiona Rae was shortlisted for the Turner Prize, and in 1993 for the Austrian Eliette von Karajan Prize. Rae was elected to the Royal Academy of Arts in 2002, and served as a Tate Artist Trustee from 2005 to 2009. The artist was appointed as the first female Professor of Painting at the Royal Academy Schools from 2011 to 2015, and in 2015 was awarded an Honorary Fellowship by Goldsmiths, University of London.

Fiona Rae has exhibited extensively at museums and galleries internationally, including the Carré d'Art – Musée d'art contemporain de Nîmes, France; Kunsthalle Basel, Switzerland; Kunstmuseum Stuttgart, Germany; Kunstmuseum Wolfsburg, Germany; Leeds Art Gallery, UK; Museum of Contemporary Art Shanghai (MoCA), China; Singapore Art Museum (SAM); Tate Britain, London, UK; Tate Liverpool, UK; Hayward Gallery, London, UK.

Rae's work is held in numerous public and private collections, including the Centre Pompidou, Paris, France; Tate Collection, London, UK; Fonds national d'art contemporain (FNAC), Paris, France; Musée d'Art Moderne Grand-Duc Jean (Mudam), Luxembourg; Fundacio La Caixa, Palma de Mallorca, Spain; Hirshhorn Museum and Sculpture Garden, Washington D.C., USA; Hamburger Bahnhof – Museum für Gegenwart – Berlin, Germany; National Museum of Women in the Arts, Washington, D.C., USA; Albertina, Vienna, Austria.

Fiona Rae lives and works in London.

Biografie

In den letzten dreißig Jahren hat Fiona Rae ein bemerkenswertes Œuvre geschaffen, das auf der konzeptuellen Auseinandersetzung mit den Fragestellungen und Möglichkeiten der abstrakten Malerei basiert. Rae erneuert ihre Vorgehensweise häufig durch selbst auferlegte strategische Herausforderungen, die bis dato zu über 15 verschiedenen Malerei-Serien geführt haben. Die Gemälde werden direkt auf der Leinwand improvisiert und legen dabei malerische sowie semiotische Codes fest, innerhalb derer jedes visuelle Element den gleichen Stellenwert und die gleiche Bedeutung in einem offenen und demokratischen, fiktiven Raum besitzt. Bekannt für ihren ikonoklastischen Umgang mit Inhalten und formalen Voraussetzungen, verkörpern Fiona Raes Bilder ein abstraktes Pop-Universum voller Anspielungen auf moderne und zeitgenössische Gemälde, Pop-Kultur und digitale Technologien.

Fiona Rae wurde 1963 in Hongkong geboren. Nach ihrem Studium am Croydon College of Art und am Goldsmiths College in London nahm Rae 1988 an der wegweisenden Ausstellung *Freeze* in den Londoner Docklands teil und wurde eine der ersten Vertreterinnen der Young British Artists (YBAs), die nicht nur die britische Kunstszene verändern sollten.

1991 stand Fiona Rae auf der Shortlist für den Turner Prize und 1993 für den österreichischen Prix Eliette von Karajan. Rae wurde 2002 an die Royal Academy of Arts berufen und war von 2005 bis 2009 Tate Artist Trustee. Die Künstlerin wurde die erste weibliche Professorin für Malerei an den Royal Academy Schools und lehrte dort von 2011 bis 2015. 2015 erhielt sie den Honorary Fellowship der Goldsmiths, University of London.

Fiona Rae hat häufig in internationalen Museen und Galerien ausgestellt, darunter Carré d'Art – Musée d'art contemporain de Nîmes, Frankreich; Kunsthalle Basel, Schweiz; Kunstmuseum Stuttgart, Deutschland; Kunstmuseum Wolfsburg, Deutschland; Leeds Art Gallery, Großbritannien; Museum of Contemporary Art Shanghai (MoCA), China; Singapore Art Museum (SAM); Tate Britain, London, Großbritannien; Tate Liverpool, Großbritannien; Hayward Gallery, London, Großbritannien.

Raes Arbeiten sind in zahlreichen öffentlichen und privaten Sammlungen vertreten, darunter Centre Pompidou, Paris, Frankreich; Tate Collection, London, Großbritannien; Fonds national d'art contemporain (FNAC), Paris, Frankreich; Musée d'Art Moderne Grand-Duc Jean (Mudam), Luxembourg; Fundacio La Caixa, Palma de Mallorca, Spanien; Hirshhorn Museum and Sculpture Garden, Washington D.C., USA; Hamburger Bahnhof – Museum für Gegenwart – Berlin, Deutschland; National Museum of Women in the Arts, Washington D.C., USA; Albertina, Wien, Österreich.

Fiona Rae lebt und arbeitet in London.

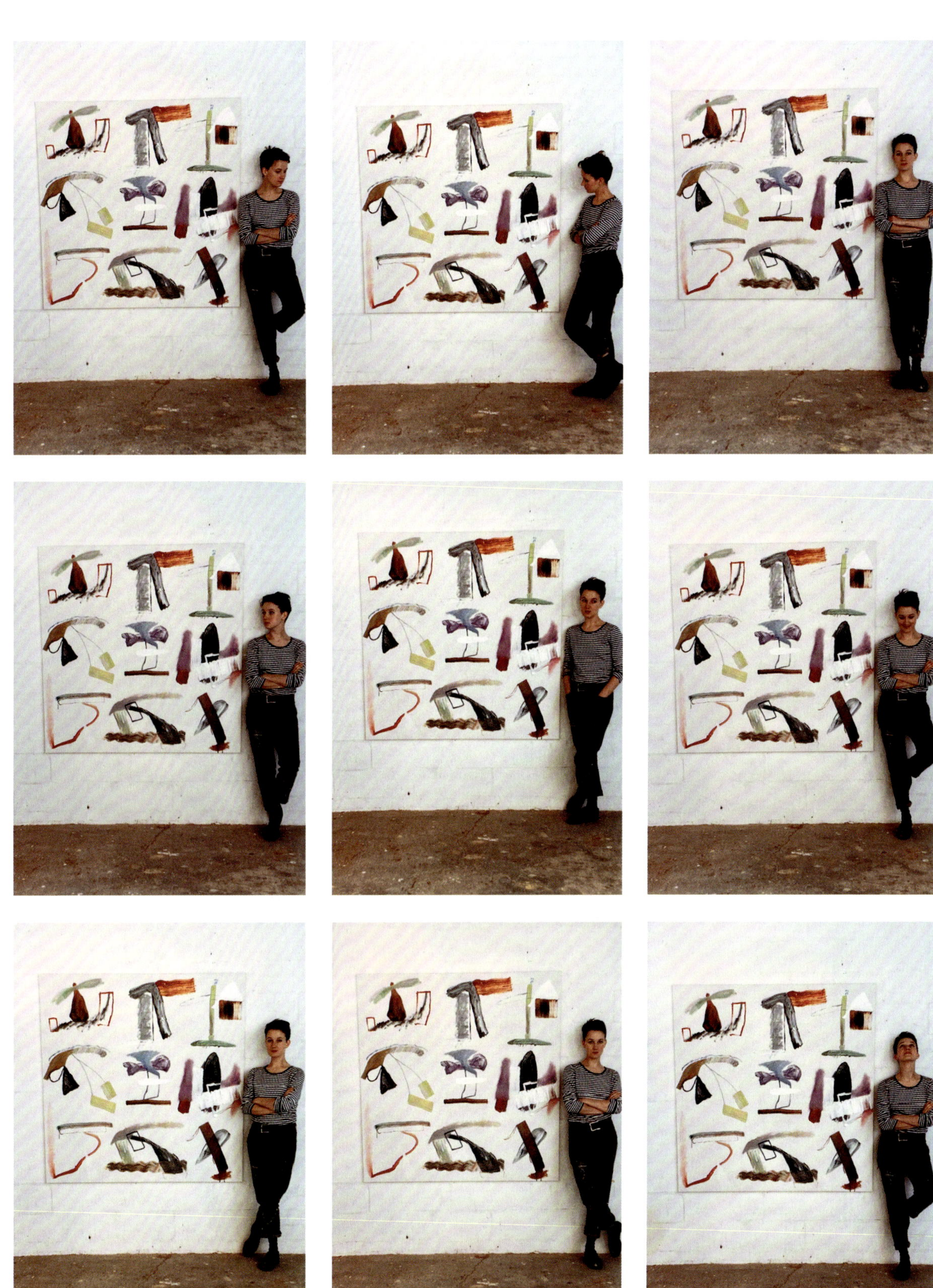

Press photos of Fiona Rae in her studio for *Freeze*, 1988
Pressefotos von Fiona Rae in ihrem Atelier für *Freeze*, 1988

Colophon | Impressum

This catalogue is published on the occasion of the exhibition
Dieser Katalog erscheint anlässlich der Ausstellung

Fiona Rae – Row Paintings
November 5 – December 18, 2021
5. November – 18. Dezember 2021

Buchmann Galerie
Charlottenstraße 13
10969 Berlin

+49 30 258 999 29
info@buchmanngalerie.com
www.buchmanngalerie.com

Editor | Herausgeber
Buchmann Galerie, Berlin

Design and production management
Gestaltung und Produktion
Peter B. Willberg, London

Managing editors | Redaktion
André Buchmann, Erik Herkrath

Essay | Text
Terry R. Myers, Los Angeles

Translation | Übersetzung
Uta Grosenick

Copy editing | Lektorat
Doris Hansmann, Katrin Höller

Image editing | Lithografie
Printmanagement Plitt GmbH

Photo credits | Fotonachweis
Antony Makinson at Prudence Cuming Associates Ltd, London
except | außer p. | S. 55: Studio Fiona Rae

Printing and binding | Gesamtherstellung
optimal media GmbH

Distribution and marketing
Vertrieb und Marketing
DCV
sales@dcv-books.com

ISBN 978-3-96912-041-5
Printed in Germany

Published by | Erschienen bei
DCV
www.dcv-books.com

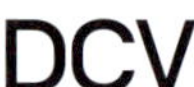

Supported by | Gefördert von

STIFTUNG KUNSTFONDS

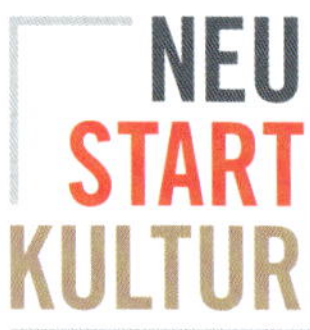